ADOPTING THE RACING GREYHOUND

ADOPTING THE RACING GREYHOUND

CYNTHIA A. BRANIGAN

Howell Book House
New York

Maxwell Macmillan Canada
Toronto

Maxwell Macmillan International
New York   Oxford   Singapore   Sydney

Howell Book House
Macmillan Publishing Company
866 Third Avenue
New York, NY 10022

Maxwell Macmillan Canada, Inc.
1200 Eglinton Avenue East
Suite 200
Don Mills, Ontario M3C 3N1

Macmillan Publishing Company is part of the Maxwell Communication Group of Companies.

Unless credited otherwise, all photographs are by the author.

Library of Congress Cataloging-in-Publication Data
Branigan, Cynthia A.
    Adopting the racing greyhound / Cynthia A. Branigan.
        p.   cm.
    Includes index.
    ISBN 0-87605-190-5
        1. Greyhounds.   2. Greyhound racing.   I. Title.   II. Title:
    Racing greyhound.
    SF429.G8B73   1992
    636.7′53—dc20   92-9627   CIP

The purpose of this book is to provide information for those adopting and caring for an ex-racing Greyhound. The Publisher and/or author shall not be responsible for any injuries or damage incurred by following the information given in this book.

Macmillan books are available at special discounts for bulk purchases for sales promotions, premiums, fund-raising, or educational use. For details, contact:

Special Sales Director
Macmillan Publishing Company
866 Third Avenue
New York, NY 10022

10 9 8 7 6 5 4 3 2 1

Printed in the United States of America

DESIGN BY DIANE STEVENSON/SNAP'HAUS GRAPHICS.

This book is dedicated, with love and gratitude, to
KING (Low Key Two)
Without whose gentle spirit and inspiration
This book could not have been written.
The work continues in his name . . .

(Photo: Ann G. Krisher)

CONTENTS

FOREWORD

It isn't every author of a foreword to a book who will tell you to beware. But I am doing so. I am not saying, mind you, to beware of the dog because this book is about one of the most endearing breeds of dog in the world. Nor am I saying to beware this book—which is one of the most thorough manuals of adoption that has ever been my pleasure to read. What I am doing, however, is saying to beware of the author.

I first met Cynthia Branigan nearly twenty years ago when she was a newspaper reporter in Philadelphia. Since that time I have known her as a friend and long-time fellow worker at The Fund for Animals. I am telling you this because The Fund for Animals specialized in the rescue of all kinds of animals—wild burros from the Grand Canyon, wild goats from San Clemente Island, wild horses, wild pigs and even the last Atlantic City Steel Pier Diving Horses. I learned early on that Cynthia, who loved all animals, was also a marvelous adopter of all animals. Indeed whatever animal we rescued, Cynthia could and would find the right person to adopt it.

I remember well the day Cynthia told me she had fallen in love with a dog. I knew she had been working with Greyhound rescue and had in fact set up her own society for that task—so I asked her if the object of her affection was a Greyhound. She said it was. His name, she said, was King. With that she poured out paean of praise and superlatives about not only King in particular and the entire Greyhound breed in general but also why everyone, man, woman and child, should have one.

I am, of course, kidding to ask you to beware this woman. Cynthia is much too much of a professional to want anyone to adopt an animal who is likely to be incompatible with that animal. Instead, as her book makes amply clear, she is just as interested in whether you are right for the dog you think you want to adopt as in whether that dog is right for you.

This book goes into virtually every conceivable situation that a person adopting a Greyhound is likely to encounter. But with its completeness the book is also extraordinarily readable, including both the proud history of this oldest of all purebred dog families as well as fascinating individual stories from people across the country who have decided for humanitarian reasons, or for the simple desire for companionship, to adopt.

Don't think I'm going to let the beware idea go completely, though. It is true Cynthia leans over backward to point out the adjustments and even difficulties you may have. But somehow in between the lines of these cautions you can read clear as crystal Cynthia's deep and abiding love for these creatures. "Don't worry," she is saying, "go ahead. You will not regret it."

CLEVELAND AMORY

ACKNOWLEDGMENTS

For their technical advice and assistance, and for their dedication to excellence in their field, the author wishes to thank the following:

John Ard, Greyhound trainer, Seabrook, NH

Lou Batdorf, Greyhound Pets of America representative, Wheeling, WVA

Nancy and Bob Checkaneck, Companion Animal Placement, Basking Ridge, NJ

Phil Hurst, operations manager, J. C. Ehrlich Co., Doylestown, PA

Dr. Alan Klide, associate professor of veterinary anesthesia, University of Pennsylvania School of Veterinary Medicine

Christine Makepeace, REGAP director, Seabrook, NH

Charlotte Mosner, Reynolds Greyhound Enterprises, Atlantic Beach, NY

Susan Netboy, Greyhound Friends for Life, Woodside, CA

Love and gratitude to:

My parents, Elizabeth and Francis Branigan, who always encouraged my interest in animals and writing

And Cleveland Amory, who helped show me the way

ACKNOWLEDGMENTS

And a "thank you" just for being there to:

Ajax, Alice, Ben Banker, George Banks, Mary Bloom, Betty and Alan Branigan, Bridget, Tom Bruno, Calvin, Clawdia, Fiona, Charlie and Gary Ford, Marge and Bill Goodman, Hamish, Leslie Holzman, Jasper, Deva Kaur Khalsa, Carol and Bruce Lazaravich, Sheryl and Jay Leeb, Bev and Roland Mostovy, Marian Probst, Deborah and Bob Rabinsky, Ramsey, Catherine and Thomas Schwartz, Daniel Stern, Charles and Anita Taylor, Anne Jill Weatherley, Barbara and Al Wicklund, JoAnne and Ed Wildman, and all the members of Make Peace With Animals

A special thanks to Sean Frawley, President of Howell Book House, who shares my enthusiasm for Greyhounds and who backed my idea for this book, and to my editor, Madelyn Larsen, who understands sighthounds and whose criticism of this book improved it greatly.

INTRODUCTION

///////////

When people harbor misconceptions about retired racing Greyhounds, they generally have one of the following: that the dogs are old pensioners with, at best, only a year or so left of life or that they, as a breed, are suited only for racing.

I'm happy to report that neither is true.

Until recently, when racing Greyhounds were finished with their careers the fate met by many was euthanasia or sale to research laboratories. Now, thanks to the efforts of adoption centers across the country, these dogs are finally having their day.

Former racing Greyhounds are, in many important ways, unlike other dogs. Even seasoned dog owners may find some of their behavior baffling. Psychologically, physiologically and even historically, these dogs are different. Consequently, methods of training and care need to be adapted to fit their special needs. It is not that they are more difficult, quite the contrary, but they are unique. If you follow the advice in this book, all of which is based on extensive research and a good deal of personal experience, you will be able to help them fit in with ease.

Most Greyhounds available for adoption range in age

from two to five years. Given that their lifespan is estimated at twelve to fourteen years, you can well expect to have a long and happy time with your ex-racer.

Racing is both highly competitive and physically demanding. Many young dogs may seem, to you, to be faster than the speed of light. But, compared to others of their breed, they don't quite measure up. These "slow" dogs, not much more than pups, may be sidelined almost before their careers begin. Other dogs may have suffered a minor injury on the track. While it probably doesn't affect them at all as a companion, it may have been enough to slow them down. In a sport where every second counts, this, too, may be a reason for retirement. Finally there are the dogs that had a full racing career. By the age of five most Greyhounds, even the superstars, have run out of steam. But, again, nearly two-thirds of their life is still ahead of them, and after all their hard work they, perhaps above all others, deserve a good retirement.

Greyhounds have, for thousands of years, been bred to do two things: run like the wind and work together with other dogs. They were not bred to be solitary hunters, and the transition from hunting to racing has kept the spirit of cooperation intact. For this reason, Greyhounds tend to get along with other dogs. Yet the muzzles worn by the racers cause some to infer that they are fighters. Not so. In Greyhound racing the dog whose nose crosses the finish line first is the winner. The muzzle helps make the nose more prominent and assists the judges in determining which dog won.

Of course, there is a safety factor involved. Whenever you have eight dogs, of any breed, in hot pursuit of something, be it a ball or an artificial rabbit, their natural desire to get the prize can cause the mildest dog to become competitive. But, once the object of their desire is removed, almost like magic they become their sweet old selves again.

Greyhounds are extremely companionable, good-natured dogs. In fact, as a breed, they seem to have a higher than average incidence of smiling. When they are very happy, such as when you get home, or when they want to play, many raise their upper lip and show their teeth. This is accompanied by wild tail-wagging and prancing. Who among us can resist such a goofy display?

There are two types of people for whom a retired racing Greyhound is ideal: those with families and those without. Let me explain.

Greyhounds, especially young males, have a great deal of patience, and most seem to understand that small children must be handled with care. If the playing gets too rough, Greyhounds tend to walk away rather than snap. Of course, children should always be supervised when playing with any dog and must be taught to respect the animal's feelings. But, as many families can attest, Greyhounds and gentle children are perfect together.

And for singles who are looking for an affectionate, loving pet, a Greyhound can't be beat. You will be rewarded many times over for whatever attention you give your dog. Greyhounds, perhaps because of their long and aristocratic history, are "to the manner born." They thrive in a home environment and take to it as if they waited all their lives for the experience. They are the sort of dog that likes keeping you within sight and have been known to follow their "person" from room to room.

In 1930, the British dog writer James Matheson praised the retired racer as a companion. He said of him, "His intelligence defies all attempts at description. There would appear to be nothing which he does not understand either in word or in gesture or the shadow of coming events. When your favourite has done his work, cherish him and give him a place with yourself for the rest of his but too short life. It is his one drawback. He should live as long as his owner."

By choosing to share your home and life with a Greyhound, you are participating in an act nearly as old as civilization itself. These are the same dogs that slept alongside the pharaohs, hunted with the noblemen of the Middle Ages, and have inspired artists and poets for thousands of years. Without a doubt they are worthy of us. The question is, Are we worthy of them?

CHAPTER

1

A BRIEF HISTORY OF THE BREED

////////////

Most dog care books devote a page, or at most two, to the history of the breed they are discussing. There's a very good reason for this: there isn't that much history to tell. The history of the Greyhound, however, is long and rich, and a brief condensation of it is important if you want to get the full flavor of just how long these dogs have been our companions.

THE GREYHOUND FAMILY

When contemplating the history of the Greyhound, it is useful to think in terms of the Greyhound family. As much as anyone may tell you that this or that breed is the oldest known to man, the truth is no one knows for sure. What we do know, however, is that the earliest pure-bred dogs were of the Greyhound-type. The Greyhound family has several characteristics in common. Among them are long legs, a long narrow head, a deep chest and the ability to hunt by sight (hence the term sighthound, or gazehound) rather than by scent as most dogs do. As this type of dog moved to different parts of the world, some of his superficial characteristics, such as the length of his coat and the shape of his ears, began to change to accommodate the conditions of his new environment.

MEMBERS OF THE FAMILY

Members of the Greyhound family that are recognized by the American Kennel Club are Afghan Hounds, Borzois, Greyhounds, Ibizan Hounds, Irish Wolfhounds, Pharaoh Hounds, Salukis, Scottish Deerhounds and Whippets. Fringe members include Basenjis and Rhodesian Ridgebacks (which hunt by sight but do not share a physical resemblance) and Italian Greyhounds (which share a physical resemblance but don't hunt at all).

THE FIRST
GREYHOUND-TYPES

The first traces of the long, lean dogs of the Greyhound-type were seen in the ancient city of Catal-Huyuk, located in what is now southwest Turkey. Temple drawings, dating to 6000

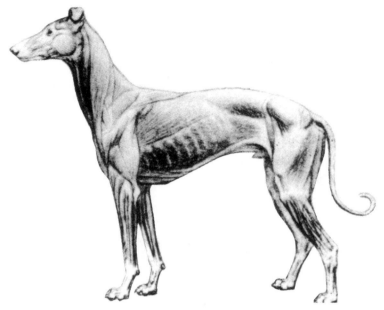

The musculature of a Greyhound.

B.C., show a hunter pursuing a stag with the help of two Greyhound-types.

As people migrated to different parts of the globe, they took their dogs with them. About 4000 B.C., in what is now Iran, a funerary vase was created that was decorated with the image of Greyhounds. Obviously these dogs were held in high regard for their image to have been added to so personal an item.

ANCIENT EGYPT

It was in Egypt, however, that the Greyhound really came into his own. Not only were the dogs kept as companions (in addition to being hunting partners), but they were practically worshiped.

The Egyptian god Anubis was, as were many Egyptian deities, half man and half beast. In this case the beast was, depending on which sources you consult, either a jackal or a Greyhound. In looking at a painting or statue of Anubis, the resemblance to the present-day Pharaoh Hound is unmistakable.

The Egyptians valued their Greyhounds so much that the birth of one was second in importance only to the birth

The Egyptian god Anubis.

of a human boy. Indeed, when a pet Greyhound died, the entire family would mourn by shaving their heads, fasting and wailing.

Greyhounds were buried, and mummified, along with their owners, and the walls of the tombs were often decorated with figures of favorite Greyhounds who had died before their owners. Among the Pharaohs who kept Greyhounds were Tutankhamen, Amenhotep II, Thutmose III and Queen Hatshepsut. Cleopatra, too, was an aficionado.

While the ancient Israelites did not worship Greyhounds and, in fact, seemed to regard dogs in general with disdain, they did make an exception for the Greyhound. It is the only breed of dog named in the Bible. Proverbs 30: 29–31 reads:

> *There be three things which go well, yea,*
> *Which are comely in going:*
> *A lion, which is strongest among beasts and*
> *Turneth not away from any;*
> *A Greyhound;*
> *A he-goat also.*

ANCIENT GREECE

When explorers from Greece traveled to Egypt, they were suitably impressed by the Greyhounds and managed to take some back with them to their homeland. The dogs' popularity caught on to such an extent that even the Greek hero Alexander the Great kept one, which he named Peritas.

The first dog mentioned in literature, in 800 B.C., was, you guessed it, a Greyhound. In the *Odyssey*, Homer told the tale of the return of Odysseus, who had been away from home for twenty years. The only one who recognized him was his Greyhound, Argus, who was only a pup when Odysseus left.

Greek mythological figures were frequently portrayed with Greyhounds. Hecate, goddess of wealth, is often shown accompanied by a Greyhound, as is Pollux, protector of the hunt. And, of course, the famous story of Actaeon and Artemis tells of the goddess taking revenge on Actaeon by turning him into a stag and setting her forty-eight Greyhounds on him.

ANCIENT ROME

The ancient Romans appropriated many things of value from Greek culture, and this included an appreciation of the Greyhound. Their gods and goddesses, too, had Greyhounds, and the most well-known story is of Diana, goddess of the hunt, who gave her best friend, Procris, a Greyhound named Lelaps. Lelaps accompanied a hunter into the woods and, when the dog spotted a hare, went off in hot pursuit. The gods watched the scene and, not wanting the hare to be killed, turned both it, and Lelaps, into stone. This scene of Lelaps chasing the hare is often depicted in Roman art.

The Romans loved to run their Greyhounds but, in even those bloodthirsty days, there was at least one person who had a vestige of humanity. In A.D. 124 Arrian wrote a treatise entitled "On Hunting Hares." He urged his readers to concentrate more on the sport and less on the gore, stating, "The true sportsman does not take out his dogs to destroy the hares, but for the sake of the course and the contest between the dogs and the hares, and is glad if the hares escape."

MEDIEVAL AND RENAISSANCE TIMES

During the Middle Ages, a time of famine and pestilence, Greyhounds very nearly became extinct. They were saved, however, by clergymen who protected them from starvation and bred them for noblemen. It was during this period that ownership of a Greyhound became the exclusive right of the nobility.

King Canute enacted a law in 1016 in England that prohibited any "meane person" from owning a Greyhound and punished any infraction severely. A hundred years earlier in Wales, King Howel decreed the punishment for killing a Greyhound was the same as for killing a person, death.

Since Greyhounds were the first breed of dog mentioned in literature, it is only fitting that they also were the first breed of dog written about in the English language. In the late fourteenth century, Geoffrey Chaucer wrote in *The Canterbury Tales*: "Greyhounds he hadde as swift as fowels in flight." Shakespeare, too, mentioned them. In *Henry V* he wrote: "I see you stand like Greyhounds in the slips, Straining upon the start. The game's afoot."

During the Renaissance, the elegant lines of the Greyhound were not overlooked by the most famous artists of the era. Among those who saw fit to immortalize these dogs in art were Veronese, Pisanello and Uccello. While Veronese's works tended toward the sacred, Pisanello and Uccello seemed to appreciate the Greyhound form for its own sake. Uccello's painting "Hunt in the Forest," for example, shows dozens of Greyhounds in a dark woods helping hunters capture their prey.

A Greyhound head by the Italian Renaissance artist Pisanello, circa 1400.

COURSING

The sport of coursing, which has its origins in ancient Greece, helped keep the Greyhound a popular animal. As coursing was originally practiced, two Greyhounds would be "slipped" (released) in a field to run after a hare that also would be released but given a hundred-yard advantage. The victor was not necessarily the dog that caught the rabbit, and, in fact, quite often the rabbit escaped. Instead, the dogs were judged by a complicated set of rules that valued such things as the dog's agility and concentration. In the mid-1700s, a set of rules was developed that helped popularize the sport and caused it to spread throughout Great Britain and across the Continent.

A modern Greyhound head shows very little change.

THE BULLDOG BREEDINGS

The mid-1700s were also important in Greyhound history for another reason: it was then that an eccentric English nobleman by the name of Lord Orford began his now-famous Greyhound-Bulldog breedings. His idea was that by breeding a male Bulldog with a female Greyhound, the result would be a dog that had a uniformly smooth coat (which had eluded breeders up until that time) and that they would possess what Lord Orford called "courage."

Lord Orford's crosses continued for seven generations, and the resulting dogs were of such high quality that those who had previously been skeptical were now clamoring to buy his dogs.

Two famous coursing Greyhounds, Riot and David, from an 1878 engraving.

ON TO AMERICA

As people from the British Isles emigrated to America, they often brought their Greyhounds with them. Coursing was a sport that was a natural for the wide-open expanses of the prairie, and the participants justified the killing of rabbits

Hecate was a second generation cross from the Bulldog breedings of Lord Orford in the mid-1700s.

with the argument that they were helping to protect the farmers' crops from hungry hares. General George Custer reportedly coursed his fourteen Greyhounds on the night before Little Big Horn. We know of Custer's unfortunate fate, but what happened to his Greyhounds remains lost to history.

Greyhound Racing—an American Sport

In the early 1900s, Owen Patrick Smith invented the artificial lure that accomplished two things at once: it allowed more people to see the Greyhounds as they were raced on

Greyhound racing is a sport made in the United States. (Photo: National Greyhound Association)

an oval track and it eliminated the need to kill live rabbits. And so, Greyhound racing was born. From those early days it has caught on in popularity around the world and is now the sixth most popular spectator sport in America.

But the history of the Greyhound is not finished yet. The one you write with your dog will be the most interesting of all.

CHAPTER

2

CHOOSING THE RIGHT DOG FOR YOU

////////////

One of the most important things you can do to foster a good relationship with your dog should take place before you even get him: choosing in advance the right dog for you.

How, you ask, can this be done in advance? Simple. Make a list of all the desirable traits you would like your dog to have. And, if a specific color is at the top of that list, you're in trouble before you even begin.

Let me explain . . .

People who adopt ex-racers usually do so by one of two methods: either they travel to a kennel that houses retired dogs or they adopt through an organization that gets a dog for them. Both methods can be perfectly suitable or fraught with peril. Adopting a dog is a serious commitment and is a decision you may live with for ten to fifteen years. It is definitely not to be entered into on a whim nor for a superficial consideration such as the dog's color. This is why I recommend a list because it can help make it clear to you exactly what you are looking for in a dog and why.

SHOULD YOU HAVE A DOG?

First, you need to give serious thought to whether or not you are ready for the responsibility of *any* dog. If you work very long hours and live in a small apartment, a cat or bird may be a better companion. Remember, too, that there is more to owning a dog than simply feeding him twice a day. Dogs need exercise, training, grooming, regular veterinary care, and lots of affection. Can you afford all of this in both time and money?

WHY DO YOU WANT A GREYHOUND?

Now ask yourself why, specifically, you want a Greyhound. Perhaps you have been caught up in the plight of the ex-racers and want to help. Helping is admirable, of course, but is adopting a Greyhound really the best way for you to assist? It's possible that you could serve the cause better by finding other people to adopt. Another possibility is to serve as a foster home for a Greyhound. That way you can provide a much-needed service for the adoption agency and get an idea of what it would be like to have one in your home. Who knows, you may wind up adopting the foster dog yourself!

There are two things about Greyhounds that could cause some people to want another breed: they are large dogs and, as ex-racers, they cannot be allowed to run off-lead except in a fenced area.

DO YOU HAVE ENOUGH SPACE?

As to the first point, even though I tell people that they are small large dogs (rather like the seeming contradiction of the name Little Big Horn), what I mean by that is that they are graceful, short-coated and often curl up in a tight ball when they sleep. Because of that they don't have as much of a physical presence as, say, a Newfoundland or a St. Bernard. They are, however, undeniably bigger than a Chihuahua or any of the many medium-sized breeds. Do you have the space for those long legs, or will you and the Greyhound constantly be tripping over each other?

WHY GREYHOUNDS CANNOT RUN LOOSE

The second point of not letting the dog run free pretty well speaks for itself; but there are so many people who adopt who think that their dog is somehow different and can be trusted not to run away, let me support the statement with some facts and a few sad anecdotes.

Greyhounds are one of the fastest land mammals, with speeds reaching 41.72 mph. Horses, by comparison, have been known to reach 43.26 mph. If you think that you will simply run and catch your Greyhound if he bolts, consider this: a sprinting man can run only 27.89 mph. Therefore, catching a running Greyhound is only slightly less difficult than catching a running horse—which is to say impossible.

Greyhounds have been bred for literally thousands of years for one thing: speed. If you think an obedience course is enough to wipe out eons of genetics and training you are deluding yourself *and* risking your dog's life. In the case of retired racers, the situation is more acute because they have had the speed/chase mentality reinforced in them from the moment they were born. And, as we all know, what we learn as a child (or puppy) is what tends to stay with us for life.

Even before I began placing retired racers, I was drawn to them for their beauty and serenity. Every October I travel to New York City to attend the Feast of Saint Francis at the Cathedral of Saint John the Divine. On that day, all animals, from the huge elephant in the procession to the household pet, are welcome inside the church. The entire service is devoted to a celebration of animal life.

Every year I talk to a man who comes all the way from Boston for the event with his two beautiful ex-racers. The dogs were so calm and loving that they used to try to sit on his lap in the pew! Last year he came with only one dog. When I inquired about the other I heard the answer I feared: the dog was dead.

Despite warnings from the person he had adopted the dogs from, the man felt he knew his dogs well enough, and had lived with them long enough (five years), that the advice to keep them on a lead no longer applied. Besides, he reasoned, the dogs had been obedience-trained. So, for several years he had been allowing them to run free in a large park in Boston well away from the park's boundaries. His version of Russian roulette worked quite well until that fateful day when a squirrel crossed the Greyhound's path. Perhaps the dog felt especially good that day. Perhaps some old chasing memory clicked inside his brain. For whatever reason, he took off and ignored the call of his owner. The boundary of the park meant nothing to the dog, and we can only hope that when he ran between two parked cars and into the path of a bus that his death was swift and painless.

Here's another tale, which, while obviously foolhardy, gives you another idea of what can happen:

A woman from Florida who had adopted a Greyhound almost a year earlier took her dog, unleashed, to a Fourth of July parade. Naturally there were crowds, the sounds of marching bands, and the occasional firecracker. It was a firecracker that so startled the otherwise calm dog that he took off. Several people tried to catch him, but his fear exceeded their speed. His dead body, obviously hit by a car, was found the next day ten miles from the parade site.

So, if you adopt a Greyhound, are you willing to keep him leashed? He can run in your fenced yard, of course. And if you don't have a fenced yard, perhaps you have a friend or neighbor who would let you release your dog once or twice a week in their yard. Another alternative is a fully enclosed tennis court, football or baseball field. If none of the above is available, let me assure you that a good brisk walk once or twice a day will more than satisfy your dog's exercise needs.

HOW TO CHOOSE YOUR IDEAL GREYHOUND

Now that you've decided that you *do* want a Greyhound, ask yourself the following (listed in order of importance):

Personality

What type of personality would you like your dog to have?

While all Greyhounds share some traits in common, there are individual differences. Do you want an extremely affectionate dog? Some people find it charming when a dog follows them from room to room, others consider it an annoyance. Do you want a very intelligent dog? If you do, make

Maddie, Rumi and Leggs, safe in a fenced yard.

sure you channel the energy into something constructive because brains left untrained can think up things to do that might not be pleasing to your sense of order. Do you want a very quiet dog? Companionable and low key to one person may add up to dull and boring to another.

Activity Level

What sort of activity level do you desire in your dog? Very peppy? A potential jogging companion? A couch potato?

Be realistic. If you adopt a very athletic, active dog with the thought that it will somehow inspire you to exercise, think about what your own "track record" has been. Do you have a basement full of exercise equipment that was bought on a whim and rarely used since? Do you have a kitchen full of dust-covered diet drinks or an unused health club membership? A very active Greyhound is not going to be happy if his only exercise is following you from the refrigerator to the recliner. If you are currently exercising regularly, then do, by all means, consider a Greyhound as a jogging companion. If, however, you expect him to inspire you, try the local gym first and see how long you stick with it.

Age

Do you have a preference as to the age of the dog?

Racing Greyhounds, because they had a relatively regimented early life, tend to mature emotionally somewhat slower than other dogs. For this reason, a two-year-old is often very much a puppy. Is that appealing to you, or would you prefer a dog that has already worked out such stages as chewing and jumping around? Also, remember that the lifespan of a Greyhound is from twelve to fourteen years. Try and imagine where you will be ten years from now. Perhaps you would be better off choosing a somewhat older dog. My experience has shown me that the older dogs—

Greyhound activity ranges from this . . .

. . . to this!

from, say, four to five years—are even more grateful for their retirement homes.

Other Pets

Do you have other pets? Does your ex-racer need to get along with your cats?

Generally speaking, other dogs are not a problem, but a small number of ex-racers see cats, birds and very little dogs as moving prey. Make sure you tell the adoption agency or the person running the kennel that your new dog must get along with your other pets. There can be no guarantees, of course, when you are dealing with animals, but the person in charge should be able to direct you to a dog that they are fairly certain will fit in with the rest of your family. And, by the way, don't think that you will somehow train a dog out

Ajax and Phoebe, an Airedale, in interbreed rapport.

of the habit of lunging for cats. When the instinct is deeply ingrained, the only homes for these few are ones without small pets. Some groups try electric shock collars to "deprogram" the dogs, but I find the method to be a cruel and extremely crude way to train. Don't try it! There are plenty of homes without small pets that are perfect for the dyed-in-the-wool chasers, so there's really no reason to force the issue!

Children

Do you have children? If you do and they are very young, will your ex-racer need to have a lot of patience?

No dog is foolproof around kids, but some seem to enjoy the activity of children while others would rather be left alone. As I said in the Introduction, most Greyhounds are

King relaxing with friends Daniel, Clawdia (foreground) and Alice (background).

inherently kind, but you must not try their patience by allowing children to do whatever they want to this or any other pet. I am not just referring to children who are overtly aggressive with pets by doing such things as pulling their ears. I also mean children who are constantly falling over or stepping on the dog, or ones who will just never let the dog rest. Dogs can't tell whether something that is annoying them is intentional or accidental, and they really don't care. All they know is that it's a source of irritation.

My experience has been that the young male Greyhounds have more tolerance for children than do the females. I believe the reason for this is that females tend to regard children as puppies. It is in their nature to discipline their own puppies when they get too boisterous, and some do the same with human children. This is usually evidenced by growling or barking when their patience has been pushed to the limit. Males, on the other hand, see children as siblings. Males play more actively, so a rough-and-tumble session is what they expect.

The presence of children in the home is a fact that you must reveal to the person handling the adoption. And if you are picking out the dog in person, by all means bring your children along so you can judge the dog's reaction to them. By the way, dogs that are good with cats and small dogs are often good with kids, too.

Companion or Protector?

Are you looking just for a companion or for a companion and protector?

By nature Greyhounds are not aggressive animals, so, for guard duty, they are not ideal. Some, however, will bark when a stranger approaches the house, and that, coupled with their size, might be enough to deter someone with an idea of breaking in. In big cities where there tend to be more guard dogs, I have noticed people watching me and my dog approach them on the street and actually crossing to the other side as we get close, and then crossing back again after we pass. This is amusing because my dogs look to *me* for protection! From adopting out these dogs I have had more than a few people tell me that they are afraid of black dogs (I personally find them to be the most beautiful). So, if you want a dog that commands respect, you might consider a black one, but please remember that they are, in fact, no more aggressive than dogs of any other color.

Size

Is size a consideration?

Think about the size of your house, your yard and even your car. The smallest female can weigh as little as the mid-forties. The largest male can reach the mid-nineties. Both cases are rare. Generally the females range from fifty to sixty pounds and the males sixty-five to seventy-five pounds.

Gender

Do you have a preference as to the gender of the dog?

Because there are already more Greyhounds than there are homes for them, responsible adoption agencies will either require you to spay or neuter your new dog, or they will have it done in advance. If altering the dog is up to you, bear in mind that it is less expensive to neuter a male than it is to spay a female. And, in case you were wondering, adult male Greyhounds are not more aloof than the females and are every bit as affectionate! The only difference between a neutered male and a spayed female is that, in most cases, the

Sophie (left), a female, and Ajax (right), a male.

males are larger. Beyond that, it's just a matter of personal preference.

If you already have a dog (either a Greyhound or any other breed) and you are planning to add a Greyhound to your family, it is generally a safe bet to have a male and female together. In those cases, it is usually the female who becomes dominant. With two females together there is sometimes a bit of jockeying for position (the same can be true of two males), but it usually works out.

Don't believe what you've heard about male dogs not getting along. I have my choice of basically any dog in the world, and I've chosen three benign males. They all live peacefully together and seem to enjoy each other's company.

Neutering helps, of course, as does the fact that there are no female dogs around for whom they could compete. The main thing to keep in mind is matching their temperaments. If they get along, then it doesn't matter what sex they are.

Color

Do you have a color preference?

As I said in the beginning, looks should be your last

Three males in harmony: Ajax (front), Jasper (left) and King (right).

consideration because, once the dog is yours, trust me, it will suddenly become the most beautiful in the world. There is a wide array of Greyhound colors including black, white, fawn (tan), cream, red (rust), many shades of brindle (striped) and white with either red, fawn, black or brindle patches. The one color you will rarely see is grey (called blue). Whether it is fact or fiction, the feeling in the racing world is that the blue dogs are not good runners. For that reason they are seldom available for adoption after retirement because most never raced to begin with! Many in the racing world also feel that the blue dogs are prone to cancer and skin problems. Again, although I could find no facts to back up the prejudice against blue dogs, it is something to consider. After all, those within the industry have had lots of experience, and they should be in a position to know which dogs are the healthiest.

ADOPTING A GREYHOUND

There are innumerable ways in which to adopt a Greyhound. As was mentioned earlier, the two methods that are most common are visiting a kennel of retired racers or having an agency choose for you. Either method is fine as long as you stick to your list of requirements.

If you visit a kennel, the people there ought to be in a position to do two things to help the adoption along. First, they should be able to direct you toward dogs that match what you are looking for. Because they take care of the dogs, they are likely to be familiar with each dog's temperament. Second, they ought to be able to give you an idea of the dog's history, most importantly his medical history.

As to the first point, tell the person in charge exactly what you want. If he or she seems to disregard your request and attempts to push a wild-eyed youngster on you when you specifically stated that you wanted a companion for your retirement years, ask to speak to someone else.

I might as well warn you right now that when it comes time to make a decision, it will be hard. Nothing is more appealing than the soulful look in a Greyhound's eyes staring at you from behind the wire mesh of a crate. My advice? Stand firm and remember what you are looking for.

As to the second point, it is very important to know your dog's medical history and it may also be useful to know something about his racing career. The inocculation record should be available, as well as the date of the last heartworm and fecal examination. And, as with choosing any dog, look for clear eyes, a clean nose and no obvious signs of illness or injury.

If you are choosing a female, try and find out if she was on hormones to prevent her heat cycle, and, if she was, try and find out for how long. If she wasn't, find out when she had her last heat.

Of course you need to know if the dog has been spayed, or in the case of males, neutered and, if so, when. It is estimated that it takes thirty days for the hormone level in a dog's body to adjust to being altered, so, especially in the case of males, allow for some of the more typical male behavior to subside gradually after neutering.

Other questions to ask are how recently the dog was retired as well as why he was retired. If he was retired because of an injury, find out what kind. This is especially important if you plan on participating in certain sports with the dog such as artificial lure coursing. The dog may be in perfect health, but some injuries may preclude certain activities. If you are simply planning to nurture a house pet, don't let a minor racing injury bother you. Most will never affect a dog who simply takes walks with his owner or even one who races around the backyard.

One other point concerning the racing career is how well the dog did on the track. Often a dog who did extremely well is treated differently (better) than the other dogs. This will sometimes affect the dog's behavior in retirement.

Take the case of Amber. While she was in the foster home awaiting adoption, she literally took over the house. She demanded to be the first one fed, she took everyone's toys away from them and she snatched the softest bed away from one of the long-time residents. When, on the rare occasion that she was reprimanded, she pouted for hours afterward. It was quite unusual for a new dog to be so bossy, but when we discovered that she she had been a champion at the track as well as the trainer's favorite, suddenly it all made sense. She was spoiled, plain and simple!

If you are choosing sight unseen, you may actually be at an advantage. This way you won't be at the mercy of all those soulful eyes. It is essential, however, that the adoption agency knows what you want and can be trusted to get it. Faults in judgment do occur, of course, and sometimes a dog can behave one way in the kennel and quite differently in a home, but try to make sure that the agency is really trying for a match and not just a placement. Make sure, too, that they are willing to take back, or exchange, a dog that just does not fit in with your lifestyle.

It is hard to generalize about what you are likely to encounter with a new dog off the track. The first thing that comes to mind, however, is a bald bottom. Many of them have had the hair worn off the back and sides of their legs from rubbing against the walls of the crates they are housed in. This is nothing to worry about. Most dogs start growing hair back within a few weeks. If the hair doesn't come in within a few months, have your veterinarian perform a blood test to see if the dog has an underactive thyroid.

Another thing that is sometimes seen is skin irritation on the chest. This is caused by blocked pores (blackheads), the result of dogs lying in the sand of the turn-out pen. The problem can be treated easily by applying warm compresses to the area then gently squeezing, or by applying an ointment from your vet. You can, of course, leave it alone, as it causes no pain to the dog.

As for personality testing, the best recommendation I can give is to go for moderation. Choose neither the most active nor the most subdued. Sometimes the overly active dog can be too much to handle for the average owner. Likewise, the overly subdued, submissive type can become panic-stricken when frightened (and it often doesn't take much to get a dog in that state). A simple, mild-mannered, uncomplicated dog generally makes the best pet.

FOLLOW YOUR HEAD AND HEART

Now that you have the ideal Greyhound (for you) in mind, here's a little advice that may seem contradictory to all I've said so far: be flexible. Try to get the most important qualities you are looking for, but if one dog catches your eye and you make a connection, give the dog a chance. Perhaps the dog is a little smaller than you wanted and maybe he doesn't seem quite as smart, but there is a lot to be said for that chemistry that sometimes occurs between a person and a dog. Go with your head *and* heart.

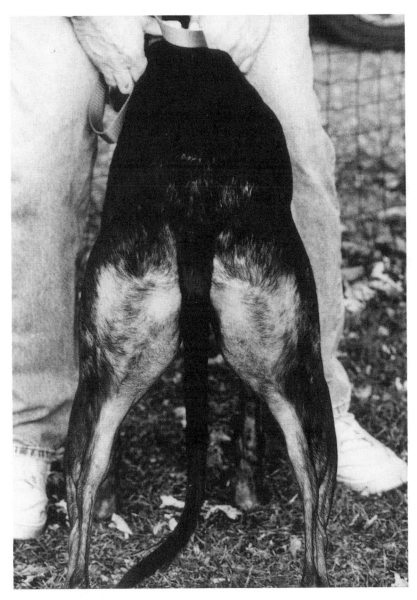

Typical baldness from crate rubbing at the track.

Choose a dog with your head and heart.

A Greyhound *will reward you with never-ending affection.*

CHAPTER 3

THE RACING LIFE

////////////

In order to understand fully why your ex-racer acts the way he does, it is helpful to know where he came from and how he is used to living life. Many of his current habits are the direct result of years of training. Knowing why he does something can assist you in changing any of his behavior that you find undesirable or in reinforcing good behavior.

THE BUSINESS ARRANGEMENTS

Racing kennels are often, but not always, located in a compound on the grounds of the Greyhound racetrack. Each kennel is owned by a different person who, in turn, hires a trainer. The kennel owners are responsible for all the bills (food, veterinary fees, etc.) that a dog incurs and for paying wages to the trainer and kennel helpers. The trainer is responsible for training a dog and for deciding which races a dog will enter and when. The owners pay nothing toward a dog's maintenance at the track, but when a dog earns money, a standard arrangement is that the kennel owner gets 65 percent of the winnings (5 percent of which is paid to the trainer), while the owner gets 35 percent. In a typical kennel, dogs from many different owners are housed and trained together.

Many owners own lots of different dogs and can have them under contract to kennels all over the country. Likewise, many owners never even meet their dogs. They can buy and sell their racers over the phone.

To a great extent, owners of a racing dog must rely on trust in the kennel owner and trainer. Often they take the trainer's word for it when they are advised to buy or sell a dog. They also must trust the kennel owner to provide proper veterinary care and nutrition for the dog. In the majority of cases, the trainers treat the dogs well in the hopes that the dogs will, in turn, perform well on the track.

THE DAILY ROUTINE

Racing kennels consist of double-deck banks of crates along the inside walls of the building with an aisle down the middle. Standard crate size is 2 ½ feet wide, 3 feet high and 3½ feet deep. The preferred bedding is shredded newspaper, since it provides both insulation and a deep cushion. Both are very important, as Greyhounds, who have very little hair and virtually no fat to act as padding, are easily chilled and prone to pressure sores when exposed to hard surfaces.

The day begins early at the track, and the same routine is repeated without variation. Generally the dogs are turned out for the first time at six or six-thirty in the morning. Three more turn-outs follow in a day: ten A.M., four P.M., and nine

Golly Wally communes with his trainer, Louis Palazzo.

Jill in her crate at the adoption kennel.

P.M. The turn-out pen is divided into two sides, one for the males and one for the females. The dogs are always turned out with their muzzles on to prevent any confrontations. As will be described in detail in a later chapter, these are not

Chris Makepeace turning out the female Greyhounds. Males are on the other side of the fence.

their racing muzzles but, rather, a smaller, lighter type used solely for turn-out and traveling.

While the dogs are relieving themselves and stretching their legs, the trainers and their helpers are busy cleaning any of the crates that have been soiled during the night. Most Greyhounds do not soil their crates, but accidents do happen.

THE HANDLING OF THE DOGS

When the dogs are brought in, perhaps thirty to forty minutes later, each one is checked before being put back into the crate. The average kennel houses about forty dogs (although there can be as many as seventy-five to one hundred), and the trainer must know each one. The length and condi-

Typical arrangement of crates. Turn-out muzzles, made of lightweight wire or plastic, hang on doors.

tion of their toenails and pads are checked, their eyes and ears are examined and, by lifting the dog into the crate and giving it the once-over, the trainer can tell if a dog is getting enough or too much to eat. Because of these frequent examinations, Greyhounds are used to being handled. Even as pups on the farm they are handled daily for such things as weighing, deworming, or being led to the turn-out pen.

THEIR MUSICAL BACKGROUND

One constant I have observed in every racing kennel is the sound of music—nonstop, twenty-four hours a day. I personally found it a bit maddening (especially some of the radio stations chosen), but I suppose you can get used to anything after a while. It was explained to me that the music serves two purposes. First, it calms the dogs and provides yet another constant in their life. Second, it helps drown out noises from the outside. If, for example, a truck pulled up during the night, all of the dogs would assume they were about to be turned out and would get up and bark. Pretty soon the entire racing compound would be awake and barking. Racing dogs need their rest, so, as strange as it may seem, the music is always on.

FEEDING

Food is extremely important in a racing kennel, both in quantity and quality. Racing Greyhounds have what is known as a set weight, which is basically the weight at which they look good and run well. Maintaining that weight is an art and a science, and there are as many different opinions on how to achieve it as there are racing kennels.

Dogs are not fed the day they are raced. A dog is not permitted to run on a full stomach because it can cause gastric torsion. Instead, dogs are given a few biscuits to tide them over until after the race.

TRAINING

By the time a dog has reached racing age, at approximately seventeen months, he has already had a good deal of training. Some of it came naturally, some was manmade.

Most racing Greyhounds are born on farms in the Midwest and in Florida. Bitches that have been bred are kept in special brooding kennels away from the other dogs. A few hours before she gives birth, the bitch makes an elaborate nest in her brooding box. Greyhounds are known for their

Trainer John Ard prepares enormous quantities of food.

keen maternal instincts, and rarely will a bitch reject her litter. Some bitches are still producing litters at ten to twelve years of age, although humane treatment would suggest an earlier retirement from motherhood. At birth, Greyhound puppies look like any other little dogs, and it is not until they are about three months of age that the distinctive long legs and long muzzle develop.

The pups are weaned by their mothers when they are eight to nine weeks old. By that age, their teeth and claws are surprisingly sharp. Although the pups are separated from their mothers, they are not separated from each other. In fact, a litter of pups, which can range in number from one to sixteen, but averages six to eight, usually remains together until they are eight to ten months old. The reason for this, in part, is because the pups help to train each other. At weaning age their ears are tattooed, which identifies them for the racing business.

At commercial breeding farms, young pups are turned out in fenced runs that are 250 to 300 feet long. As young as two months, pups begin racing with each other up and down the length of the runs. In good weather they are out for twenty to thirty minutes at a time, and if you watch them closely, you can see them already competing with each other.

At six months of age their training begins in earnest. Most trainers start out by tying a plastic jug to a rope, pulling it along the ground, and having the pups chase it. Later on, a jug or an animal pelt is pulled along by a slow-moving tractor. Still later the dogs run after an artificial lure suspended on a whirligig, and finally, they run in simulated race track conditions. Although it is illegal in most states to train the Greyhounds on a live lure, such as a rabbit, the practice still persists in some quarters. Some old-time dog trainers swear that until a dog has tasted blood he's no good

At nine weeks of age, a Greyhound pup doesn't look much like a Greyhound!

at the track. Of course, such cruel myths have no basis in fact, to which racing records will attest.

A Greyhound first gets a collar around his neck at four months of age. From the age of about eight months, Greyhounds learn to walk on a lead. The reasons for this early training are obvious: their entire lives are spent being led from one place to another. With so many dogs to handle, a trainer cannot waste time with a dog that pulls or stops frequently. This training holds them in good stead when they become companions, too.

THEIR FIRST RACE

The first professional race a Greyhound competes in is called his maiden race. Maidens are reserved for dogs, males or females, that have never won a race before. Typically races have eight dogs, but occasionally there are nine. The average age is eighteen months.

Speed is not the only factor that determines which dog will win. A dog must possess endurance and agility, too. If a dog bursts from the starting box with all of his might and holds no energy in reserve, he may well finish last. A dog must also concentrate on the lure and, simultaneously, keep his eyes on the other dogs so he doesn't accidentally bump into them. A pileup on the track could result in serious injuries and, of course, slows everyone down. Finally, a dog must not be guilty of interference, which means that he must not purposely bump other dogs or start fights with them.

A young Greyhound is given six chances to come in first, second, third, or fourth in a maiden race. If he has not achieved it by then, he is either "retired" and put up for adoption or is euthanized. I wonder how many of the betting

(Left to right) King (Low Key Two) and his littermate
Tim (Counterpoint Two), shown here with turn-out
muzzles, both ran and won in Grade A at major tracks.
(Photo: Charlotte Mosner)

public know that a young dog's very life can depend on
whether he wins, places or shows in a race.

ASCENDING THE RANKS

Assuming that all goes well and that a dog finally wins a
maiden race, he is then promoted to Grade J, which is for
dogs that have just won the maiden. Other grades, from A
to D, depend on how a dog places after each race he runs.
Generally speaking, a dog gradually ascends the grades,
then, as he ages and slows down, descends. The difference
in speed, by the way, between a Grade A dog and a Grade D
dog can be as little as ¾ of a second.

49

A veterinarian is present at each race and is responsible for all the dogs that are running. His duties can range from setting a broken leg to putting a dog to sleep to treatment for heat exhaustion.

KEEPING RACING HONEST

Every dog that wins a race has his urine analyzed for the presence of illegal drugs. Forbidden substances include butazolidin (an anti-inflammatory), stimulants, depressants, steroids and even aspirin. Ninety-seven drugs can be detected by the tests, the object of which is to keep racing honest. In addition to the winner, one other dog is picked at random after each race to be tested.

Racing bitches are every bit as fast as the dogs. To prevent them from going into heat (which would not only slow them down but would cause the dogs to riot back at the kennel), they are given testosterone. When their racing careers are over and they are taken off the hormone, many females go into heat immediately while others never go into heat again.

Usually there are thirteen to fifteen races in a day, and an individual dog is run only once every three to four days. By the time a dog reaches the finish line he has burned up all the available carbohydrates in his body. R&R is greatly needed.

At the finish line the dogs, wearing no collars, only racing muzzles and numbered blankets, are caught by the person who led them onto the track and are handed over to someone from the dog's kennel. The dog is walked a few minutes to cool down and is taken back to the kennel to rest and drink water. An hour or so after the race the dog is fed.

In most kennels, a dog that has won is given a special treat. The ones that don't win are, literally, in the dog house.

RACING INJURIES

There are several hazards that face a racing dog on the track. Some injuries can lead to their retirement, while others can lead to death. When you consider the tremendous speeds that these dogs can reach, it is a wonder that broken legs are not more common. With luck, and proper veterinary care, a leg can be set and a dog can eventually resume racing. For others, though, a break can be so severe that they can never race again. Some injuries are caused by dogs bumping into each other and others are caused by unsafe track conditions. Perhaps the worst accident possible for dogs is when they are electrocuted by falling into the cradle that holds the electric lure. Thankfully, this is a relatively rare occurrence.

Other common injuries are torn ligaments, broken bones, pulled tendons, dislocated toes and various cuts, scrapes and bruises. One injury peculiar to Greyhound racing is known as spikes. Spikes occur by accident during the course of a race when the toenail of one dog punctures the back of the leg or foot of another dog. If untreated the puncture can become infected, but, when treated properly, it is a minor, albeit painful, mishap.

When you adopt an ex-racer, try to find out exactly why he was retired. If he just wasn't fast enough, that's one thing. But if he was retired due to an injury, it may prevent him from participating in certain activities. This is especially important if you want to adopt a dog to accompany you while jogging or to take lure coursing.

*Racing Greyhounds can reach speeds over 40 mph.
(Photo: National Greyhound Association)*

IN SUMMARY

From this chapter, you now know certain things about how racing dogs live and are trained. To sum up, the following generalizations can be made:

- Racing dogs are used to rising early.

- Racing dogs are used to a strict routine.

- Racing dogs are used to being handled.

- Racing dogs are used to music.

- Racing dogs are used to walking obediently on a lead.

- Racing dogs are used to being around other Greyhounds.

- Racing dogs are used to four turn-outs daily.

- Racing dogs are used to being around people.

Remember, the more you know about your dog's past, the better equipped you will be to give him the best future possible.

CHAPTER
4
IN
A
HOME

////////////

When bringing a retired racer into your home for the first time, the one thing to keep in mind is that *everything* is completely new to him. I don't just mean that the surroundings are unfamiliar, I mean that being in a house is a new experience. Also new is riding in a car (as opposed to a kennel truck), being around more people than dogs, climbing stairs, looking out windows, adapting to your routine and a myriad of other things that we regard as commonplace.

Racing Greyhounds lead a very insular life. From the time they are born until the day you bring them home, the only life they know is that of the kennel. They might as well be from another planet as far as their knowledge of the "real" world goes. Take heart, though. Greyhounds are not only very intelligent animals, they are also very intuitive. As such, their adjustment period is probably shorter than it would be for other breeds.

SEPARATION ANXIETY

As I said earlier, Greyhounds are dogs that have been bred to get along with other animals. Consequently they tend to blend in with other pets that you might have. However, if you have no other pets, particularly no other dogs, being alone may be a little scary for your Greyhound. You see, never before have they been without other dogs, and sometimes they are initially overwhelmed by the fact that there is no other canine to reassure them.

In most cases, the Greyhound will transfer his desire for companionship to you. In practical terms, what this means is that you can expect the dog to follow you from room to room until he becomes accustomed to his new home and the routine. My dog King was so intent on keeping me within sight that for the first few months he would even follow me into the bathroom! At the time he was the only dog I had. By the time I adopted my second Greyhound, Ajax, I not only still had King, but I had also adopted a stray Afghan Hound named Jasper.

TWO'S COMPANY

I suspect that the reason Ajax never clung to me as much as King did is because he came into a multi-dog family. Don't get me wrong—Ajax is very affectionate and would always choose to be with me rather than stay home, but he never exhibited a *need* for my company, merely the desire. If you

Most Greyhounds are comforted by the presence of other dogs.

are having excessive difficulty acclimating your new Grey-hound to being left alone, do consider getting another dog, preferably another Greyhound. It may seem inconceivable to you if you are having trouble with one that getting another will actually be easier, but, believe me, it often works won-ders!

In an ideal world, we could all stay home with our dogs and never have to leave them. In reality, though, most of us go out to work. What does this mean to a dog that is unsure of himself? That all depends on how you approach your absences.

HOW NOT TO BEGIN

Let me give you the worst-case scenario first.

A couple adopts a Greyhound, fresh off the track, on a weekday afternoon. They spend the evening with the dog *and* half the neighborhood who always wanted to see what a Greyhound looked like up close. The dog is given pizza by a child, whose parents thought it was funny. The couple, in all the commotion, forgets to take the dog out, so he lifts his leg against the wall. The dog is hit hard with a newspa-per. Because the dog seems so subdued the next morning, the couple decides it's okay to allow him the run of the house when they go to work.

When they get home they find that not only was the dog not housebroken, but that he has eaten their bedspread and clawed the doors to shreds. He has drunk water from the toilet, which contained a cleaning solution that caused him to vomit on the sofa. He has also knocked the dishes from the drainboard in the kitchen onto the floor (cutting himself in the process), and has left a trail of blood all over the house. At this point the dog is in a weakened condition and requires immediate veterinary care.

HOW TO AVOID PROBLEMS

Where did the couple go wrong?

The entire problem could have been avoided by the use of a dog crate.

In adopting out retired racers, I cannot stress strongly enough to people how the use of a crate will make their lives easier as well as ease the transition for their new dog. I don't know how many times I've been asked, "But isn't it cruel to keep a dog confined?" My answer is the same every time: "Isn't it more cruel to subject a dog to the many hidden hazards around an unfamiliar house? Isn't it more cruel to return the dog after a few days because you've found him unmanageable?" To paraphrase Robert Frost, "Good crates make good dogs."

HOW TO MAKE A GOOD START

Now here's how the above scenario should have gone.

A couple adopts a Greyhound, fresh off the track, on a weekday afternoon. They spend a quiet evening with the dog, allowing him to get used to them and his new surroundings gradually. Although all of their friends and neighbors are eager to stop by and meet the new addition to the family, the couple decides that the dog has enough to contend with just checking out his new home.

The dog is given a medium-sized dinner and plenty of water, since dogs that have been recently transported are often dehydrated. The dog is taken out often, including within twenty minutes of eating and right before bed. Each time he defecates or urinates outside he is praised. If he does have an accident in the house he is told "No" firmly but without anger or shouting. He is never beaten for an accident.

Knowing that the dog is a little scared by all of the changes, the couple sets up a crate in their bedroom. The dog cries and whimpers initially, but after a half hour or so he quiets down and they all go to sleep.

The couple has arranged to take the next few days off from work—first the wife for two or three days, then the husband. That way the dog can get to know both of them equally and they can show him the ropes. Whenever they have to go out during the day without him, they put him in the crate, which is brought into the kitchen or living room during the day. Fresh water is always available in the crate. As time goes on and they are sure the dog is housebroken and will not destroy the house if left alone, the dog is weaned from the crate gradually.

That is an ideal scenario. Sometimes, however the ideal is impossible. What if, for example, the couple was unable to take time off from work? Or if someone in the family was sick when the dog arrived? In that case, perhaps someone can look in on the dog during their lunch break. Or maybe a friend or neighbor can help out. If that isn't possible, you can advertise for (or ask your vet to recommend) a dog walker. Retired people often welcome the extra money and are glad for something to do. Also, music or a talk show left playing on the radio is often soothing to the new dog. Just do the best you can, introduce things gradually to your dog and, above all, have patience.

Again, in the case of my most recent arrival, Ajax, I used the following method of allowing him free rein in the house. The first four nights he slept in the crate. By the way, the first night, as soon as I opened the door to the crate he practically ran in. The second night he walked in. The third night he walked in very slowly, and on the fourth night he needed a small push.

By the fifth night I had observed him enough to know that he could be trusted to neither chase the cats nor fight with the other dogs. I told him he could sleep uncrated on a trial basis. He was perfect and has not spent a night in a crate since.

Since I work at home I had a fairly easy job with him. He would be uncrated during the day except when I had to go out. After four or five days I began leaving him uncrated for very short periods, such as the ten minutes it would take me to get a quart of milk at the corner store. The next day I would try him uncrated for twenty minutes while I ran a few errands. Within about ten days I felt comfortable enough to leave him alone uncrated for several hours. So far he has never betrayed my trust.

CRATES

There are two basic types of crates: hard molded plastic (the kind used for transporting dogs by air) and wire (often collapsible). Either type is fine. I have heard of some people being advised that the plastic crates do not provide enough ventilation. Nonsense! They have a full-size wire door plus wire slats on the sides for ventilation. Many also have holes in the back, too. A dog should never be left in the sun in either type of crate.

An advantage of the plastic crate is that they're less expensive, usually by about $30 or $40. They're also more cavelike, which many dogs enjoy. Wire crates provide better visibility for the dog and, as was noted, are easier to store, since they are collapsible. I strongly recommend that you

Maddie enjoys getting away from it all in her crate.

buy one from a wholesale, or near wholesale, dealer, as you can save up to 50 percent of the standard retail price.

Most Greyhounds need a crate of the following dimensions: 27 inches wide by 40 inches deep by 30 inches high. Some of the smaller females, those under fifty pounds, can use the next size down (24 inches wide by 36 inches deep by 26 inches high). If you get one much bigger than is actually needed, you will increase the chances of the dog's soiling his crate because he will have enough room to move away from the mess.

Weaning from the Crate

All of the above must be combined with the rarest of commodities, common sense. If, when you feel the dog is trustworthy, you decide to leave him alone uncrated, you must

Sophie in her wire crate.

make sure that the house is relatively dog-proof. Don't leave anything of value lying around or anything that could potentially harm your dog. Scan each room in your house before you leave. If there is an irreplacable photo of Great-Aunt Bertha on the coffee table, move it. Is that a can of caustic drain opener beneath the sink? Move it. Use your imagination as to what might interest your dog. You can be sure *he* will!

The first night with your dog will undoubtedly be the hardest. Many dogs cry with anxiety. Don't worry, eventually they stop. And it's only natural that a dog will express to you that he is feeling worried. Be kind, have compassion and put yourself in his situation. Wouldn't you be worried if matters were reversed and suddenly you were forced to live in a kennel surrounded by dogs and no people?

OTHER CHALLENGES

Four things that may be obstacles to new Greyhounds are smooth or highly waxed floors (such as in the kitchen), windows, swimming pools and stairs. If you approach each obstacle with understanding, it won't be an obstacle for long.

Smooth Floors

Apparently Greyhounds never walk on really smooth floors during their racing days. The surfaces in and around the kennel and track are mostly dirt, clay or sand. Some Greyhounds walk on smooth floors without a hitch. For others, however, it appears to be a terrifying ordeal.

My own kitchen floor is linoleum, although not terribly smooth and certainly not very shiny. Neither of my Greyhounds has any trouble with it. However, when I take Ajax with me to give speeches about Greyhound adoption to service organizations and clubs, the meetings are often held in municipal buildings with very smooth, highly polished floors. The first time we went out in tandem I'm afraid he didn't come off as a very good "AmbassaDog.®" As we entered the hall it was as if Ajax was walking on ice. All four legs splayed out, and he had a lot of difficulty just standing upright, much less walking. With much coaxing, and with the use of a blanket on the floor, I was able to inch him across the room to the podium. Now he has the hang of it and could probably race around the room if given half a chance.

If your dog has trouble on smooth floors at home, get pieces of scrap carpeting that he can walk on. Scatter the patches on the floor so that there are small carpet-free areas that he must use. Gradually, over the course of the next few days, remove the pieces of carpet one by one and you probably won't need them again. There is also a resin-based product on the market that you can spray on your dog's pads to help him get a better grip. I doubt it will ever become necessary to use it, but if your dog is having an especially hard time, this product is available at pet supply stores.

This may be a good time to check the length of your dog's toenails. Usually they are kept fairly short for racing, but it's possible that they have grown too long. It is very difficult for a dog to walk properly if his toenails are untrimmed. It throws the weight of the foot toward the heel and allows him less maneuverability. Unless you are an expert, I recommend taking him to your local grooming parlor for a trimming. An appointment is often unnecessary, it only costs a few dollars, and your dog will feel better and walk better. Once you learn how to do it, a biweekly trimming will keep them in fine shape. You can also ask your

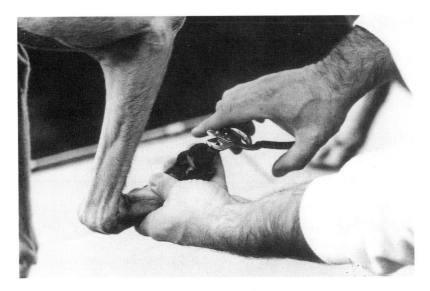

The correct way to trim toenails.

veterinarian to trim your dog's nails during an office visit. Most will do it gratis.

WINDOWS

At the racetrack, and in a kennel environment, racing Greyhounds have limited opportunity to actually look out a window. I'm not suggesting that they are kept in the dark, but they are generally either outside exercising or in the kennel building. Once inside, they mostly have a view from their crate onto an aisle facing other dogs. In the kennel trucks in which they are transported there are no windows, only louvers that can be opened for ventilation.

Because of this, windows are a new experience for your

dog, and many are delighted with their expanded view of the world. It's hard to imagine how windows could pose a threat, but they can. Here are two examples of the many I've heard.

Before I adopted King he had been in several other adoptive homes. In the first home he had a near-fatal accident involving a window. He had only lived there two days when he was running around the house playing with the other dogs. In his excitement, King ran right through a sliding glass door because he didn't recognize it as something solid. He managed to sever an artery in his leg, and his owners got him to the vet just in time to save his life. He bears the scar to this day.

In another incident, a retired racer in North Carolina by the name of Logan leapt through a bedroom window in pursuit of a squirrel that was outside. She, too, was unaware of the fact that windows are solid. Fortunately she was unharmed, and I think her owner was more shaken by it than she was.

The point here is that it's a good idea to introduce your dog to any windows that they have even a remote chance of leaping through. The simplest way to teach them is simply to lead them over to the window and knock on it. You may also want to put their nose or paw against it so they can actually feel that it is solid. Some people have put stickers or opaque tape on their windows but I have found that the knocking/touching method works quite well. By the way, don't forget car windows!

Swimming Pools

In-ground swimming pools are very common in some parts of the country. Naturally, Greyhounds are unfamiliar with them and, as with windows, they need a guided tour in order to avoid a potentially fatal mishap. Like all dogs, Greyhounds can swim, but the water level must be high enough so that they can climb out. A dog that is frightened may not be able to tread water for very long.

If you allow your Greyhound to run in a yard next to an in-ground pool, walk the dog over to the pool and make sure he understands that it contains water and is not a solid surface. This also applies to in-ground indoor pools. One of our foster homes has an indoor lap pool and a drenched Greyhound was very surprised when he discovered he couldn't walk on water! Fortunately his temporary owners were there to help him out.

Covered pools are no less of a hazard. People who are good swimmers have been known to drown in covered pools if they fall through; disorientation seems to set in almost immediately. The same applies to dogs, so make sure they understand that the cover is, at best, a flimsy surface and that water is underneath.

The best solution is to erect a fence around the pool and to keep that area off limits to your dogs.

Stairs

And now, for a match *not* made in heaven: Greyhounds and stairs. This is a tricky subject because dogs adapt to stairs in various ways. One thing is for certain, almost all of them exhibit some degree of trepidation. I believe there are two reasons for this. One is that stair-climbing is something new. The second reason has to do with their anatomy. Greyhounds are, quite obviously, very tall dogs. When you combine that with the highly developed muscles in their legs, you have an animal that bends somewhat differently from other dogs. He is built for flat-out racing, and the bulky leg muscles are something of a hindrance when it comes to steep inclines or declines. Also, the relatively short risers and narrow treads of most stairs make it very difficult for long-legged dogs.

Here's what you can do to make it easier for your dog. First of all, as was suggested for smooth floors, make the surface of your stairs as slip-free as possible. Get rubber or carpeted stair treads. Also, keep the stairs well lit, because it's always easier to accomplish anything when you can see what you're doing.

Be gentle and patient with your dog. You may find his fear of stairs silly, but it's very serious to him. Whatever you do, don't force him. You may wind up traumatizing him and turning what could have been a simple training job into a major production.

It's ideal if there are two people available to coax him up the steps—preferably close to the wall for security. One person can *gently* tug on the leash while the other can *gently* push from behind. If you have to go it alone, assume the rear position. It's futile to attempt to pull the dog up the steps by his leash. It reminds me a lot of the days when I was adopting out wild burros rescued from the Grand Canyon and Death Valley by The Fund for Animals. Before we learned the right way to do it, we would often attempt to pull the burros into the van. Needless to say, we failed. The burro would simply sit down, and that was the end of it. It wasn't until we learned to wrap the lead rope behind the hind legs and inch him forward that we made any progress. I applied this principle to Greyhounds and, presto, it worked! Put one of your arms behind the dog's rear legs, just above the hock, and nudge him forward. To descend, repeat the process, taking great care not to push him down the steps.

Quite often the Greyhound will take the steps three or

Alexandra is helped up the stairs.

more at a time. That's okay—at least he's moving forward! Eventually he will learn that he can relax going up and down steps and will take them one at a time.

If you have narrow, winding, or steep steps (I have all three) it's going to take longer for the dog to get acclimated. Again, just be patient. Once the dog realizes that he's missing out on some good times by not climbing steps, he'll make an extra effort. As always, when he is successful give him lots of praise.

CREATING A SECURE ENVIRONMENT

The final piece of advice I have for acclimating your new addition to the family is to give him a special place of his own. He will have his crate, of course, and some people choose to make it available by leaving the door open long after the dog actually "needs" it. But eventually you will want him to get more into the swing of things. What often does the trick is his own soft dog bed or a plump comforter. He will soon recognize it as his own spot and become quite attached to it. From that vantage point he can watch his new family and figure out just where he's going to fit in.

CHOOSING THE BEST VETERINARIAN

There are a few other things you should do in advance of the dog's arrival. First of all, if you don't already have a veterinarian, now is a good time to interview some. Just because you have one located near where you live doesn't mean he or she is the best choice for your dog. Call and ask if the veterinarian has other Greyhounds as clients. If not, what about other sighthounds (Afghans, Borzois, etc.). As you will learn in later chapters, sighthounds really are different, and you don't want to use a vet who is treating one for the first time. If possible, get the adoption center to recommend a good, qualified veterinarian in your area. Even if

King relaxing in his bed.

you have to drive a little farther, it's worth it to get a suitable doctor.

I also recommend that you do some comparison shopping as to the vet's rates. One man who adopted a Greyhound from me recently was charged double what my vet charges just for a basic office visit! All tests and shots were extra, of course. Look for a veterinarian who is knowledgeable about sighthounds, has a humane outlook and offers good rates.

Even if your Greyhound comes to you spayed or neutered and fully inoculated, I suggest taking him to your veterinarian for a checkup. Most adoption kennels are overworked and it is possible that they did not have the time or the staff to give your dog a complete examination. Besides, it's a good idea for your vet to see your dog at least once when he is well, so that if he becomes ill, there will be a point of comparison.

GET YOUR SUPPLIES IN ADVANCE

Finally, before your dog arrives, get in a supply of food, feeding and water bowls, a collar and leash (if they are not provided), a crate and a soft bed. That way, when you bring your dog into his new environment you can spend your time getting to know him and not have to dash out to go shopping. There's no sense letting anything interfere with the wonderful adventure you two are about to embark on together.

CHAPTER

5

CARE

AND

FEEDING

/ / / / / / / / / / / /

In Chapter Two, we discussed the importance of a good diet for a racing dog. However, since your dog is no longer a professional athlete, what should he be fed now?

First, let's examine exactly what racing dogs are fed at the track. The idea here, of course, is not to duplicate it but, rather, to diverge gradually from that regimen. If you change your dog's diet too quickly, he is likely to experience anything from mild gastric disturbances (such as gas) to diarrhea.

THE TRACK DIET

The emphasis at the race track is on performance, and in order to foster it, racing Greyhounds are fed a high-protein, high-carbohydrate diet. Protein, of course, is good for muscle development, and carbohydrates provide energy for the long haul.

Compared to other breeds of dog, Greyhounds at the track are fed enormous quantities of food. Because they burn off so many calories during a race, it would be easy for them to lose a lot of weight. The trainers compensate by feeding them an extra amount of food. Typically, the males are fed two and a half pounds a day, and the females, two pounds.

Each kennel has its own recipe, but the basics always include raw beef mixed with a high-protein dry food. Added to that can be vegetables (often spinach or turnip greens for extra iron), corn oil (for the coat), salt (to replace what is lost during a race), water (to compensate for the extra salt), powdered vitamins and electrolytes. Bowls of water are kept filled in each crate.

INTRODUCING NEW FOOD

The first item we can omit from your dog's new diet is raw beef. Not only can it be rather unpleasant to deal with, but also he doesn't need it. If you want him to have meat, substitute a good, high-quality canned dog food that doesn't contain meat by-products. If you knew what those by-products really were, you'd never feed them to your dog.

Incidentally, dogs can get by quite well on dry dog food alone. It is, after all, nutritionally balanced. However, I recommend making additions to it in part for variety and in part for added nutrition. If you are just feeding dry food, start with four cups per day for the females and five cups per day for the males (half in the morning, half in the evening), see how your dog's weight responds, and adjust accordingly.

Since your dog is no longer racing, you can downgrade from a high-protein dry dog food to one that is for normal adult maintenance. When your dog reaches the age of seven, you might want to consider the lower-protein varieties for the "mature" dog. Whatever your dog's age, you should go for a high-quality food for a number of reasons. One, the quality brands are often concentrated, which means you don't have to feed as much. Two, they aren't loaded with fillers or the dreaded "meat by-products." Three, good dry dog food tends to harden the stool, making your clean-up job a lot easier. Four, it is also better for teeth than soft foods or meat alone. And, finally, you will be giving your dog the best ingredients, which, in turn, will keep your dog healthier.

As for which brand to use, I recommend trying several kinds and seeing how your dog fares. I started off using one well-known premium brand until I discovered that it was giving two of my three dogs gas. I switched brands and the gas never came back. Other people I know use that particular brand and their dogs are fine. Each dog's metabolism is different, just as every person's is. There is no one ideal food that is perfect for every dog. Experiment and see which yours likes and which agrees with him.

CONTINUE WITH VEGETABLES

I am very much in favor of continuing the track's practice of giving Greyhounds vegetables. Dogs are omnivores, not carnivores. What this means is that in the wild dogs do not eat only meat (as do cats). Dogs eat grasses and other greens, and I believe we do them a great disservice by limiting their diet to meat.

If cooking vegetables is too much for you, try the canned

varieties. My dogs love them all, especially stewed tomatoes, carrots, broccoli, and spinach. Avoid potatoes, as dogs seem to have a hard time digesting them. Scraps from your plate are also good, not as a substitute for a balanced canine diet, but as a supplement. Cooked rice (white or brown) is also a nice addition to their diet and can be helpful in firming up loose stools.

COOKING FOR YOUR DOG

To cut down on preparation time, I cook for my dogs one day a week and simply dole out refrigerated portions. I change vegetables every week and always combine two, such as carrots and spinach. I also cook up a big batch of rice or noodles as well as a few pounds of ground beef and some beef broth. Every now and then I add a heaping teaspoon of low-fat cottage cheese, both for variety and for the extra calcium. At feeding time (twice a day) I give them a cup or so of the vegetable/rice/beef mixture with one and a half cups of dry food. I put a little warm water on the whole thing to bring the refrigerated food up to room temperature and to make it all taste better.

There are a few staples that you can have on hand to add to your dog's food that do not require a lot of work. I am rarely without a container of cottage cheese, a can of mixed vegetable juice, a jar of wheat germ, various cans of vegetables and, of course, some sort of cooked grain (rice, barley, millet, etc.). Incidentally, the mixed vegetable juice does wonders for plain dry dog food!

Don't feel that you must cook for your dogs. It's something that I enjoy doing and that I feel provides a little better quality than the commercial food available. Some people have accused my dogs of eating better than I do, and that may well be true!

PROS AND CONS OF OIL

I would add oil to a dog's food only if his coat looked dry. Otherwise you are simply adding empty calories, and all that extra fat is no better for your dog than it is for you. Also, if your dog has a tendency toward loose stools, omit the oil, as it will only aggravate the condition. If you ever need to add oil for a dry coat, the best kind to get is one high in essential fatty acids. These are generally found in fish oils (cod liver oil, for example) and provide the most complete nutrition and absorption. A few tablespoons a day will do until the coat is back in shape. A lot of all-purpose oil that people add to their dog's food simply passes through the animal's system without doing any real good.

VITAMIN SUPPLEMENTS

Once the dog is finished racing, electrolytes can be omitted from his diet. Vitamins, however, are a different story. If you take vitamins yourself, you may want to give them to your dog, too. But if the food your dog is getting says "nutritionally complete" on the label (and it should), then extra vitamins may be unnecessary. On the other hand, if you are anything like me, you may want to give your dog vitamins just for good measure. It is generally a good idea to give balanced canine multivitamins as opposed to adding specific ones. Such a practice may add too much of a particular nutrient. My younger Greyhound gets one chewable tablet daily, and the older fellows get a powdered variety for geriatric dogs mixed in with their food. It makes me feel good to give it to them, and, who knows, it may make them feel good, too!

HOW MUCH IS ENOUGH?

Many dogs that are just off the track need a little fattening up. Most people love this process, and so do the dogs. Be careful, though, not to give them too much of a good thing. Greyhounds are lean by nature, and overweight ones can develop joint trouble or arthritis from carrying around more pounds than their frame can handle. A good rule of thumb is that you should be able to feel your Greyhound's ribs easily, but you should not be able to see the outline of them. In the case of convalescing dogs that need to be coaxed into eating, I've found that raw egg yolk (never the white, which destroys the dog's B vitamins) mixed with a little evaporated milk provides lots of nourishment, is easy to digest and is highly palatable. Also, beef tea—a broth made from round steak—is often quite tempting.

One last note about food: I never recommend giving your dog the individually wrapped burger-type semimoist food. Not only are they filled with salt, sugar and artificial coloring, but they offer little more than empty calories. They will promote bad teeth, indigestion, and obesity.

KNOW YOUR DOG'S MEDICAL HISTORY

Every adoption agency has its own policy concerning what condition a dog is in when you receive it. Some dogs have had no inoculations at all. Some have had their shots but were not tested for heartworm or other parasites. Some have had everything, including spaying or neutering, teeth cleaning and even a pedicure! When you get your dog, be sure you know exactly what was done and when. This is extremely important for several reasons.

If you have other pets, you would be wise to isolate your new Greyhound from them unless he has had all of his shots. The chance that he has an infectious disease is slim, but why risk it at all? Many racing kennels do not inoculate their dogs after the first year on the theory that since they are associating only with each other, they cannot pick up any illnesses. This, of course, is shortsighted. Some diseases, such as parvovirus, are airborne. Others, such as rabies, could be transmitted if a rabid raccoon somehow wandered into a kennel's turn-out pen and bit a dog. On the East Coast in 1991 we had a virtual rabies epidemic, so it is essential that these dogs be protected immediately.

TAKE YOUR NEW DOG FOR A CHECKUP

Within twenty-four hours of taking custody of your new Greyhound, he should be seen by a veterinarian if he has not already been immunized. Also, at that time have him checked for heartworm and, if possible, get him on a monthly preventative pill. And, finally, bring a fecal sample along. If he does have worms it will not only be debilitating to his health, but some kinds can be picked up by your other pets. Some types of parasite infestation can be deadly, so this is not a condition to be taken lightly. See Chapter Six for specific recommendations on deworming preparations.

SPAYING AND NEUTERING

Your visit to the vet is a good time to set up an appointment for the dog to be spayed or neutered if it hasn't been done already. It cannot be overemphasized how important this is. With tens of thousands of Greyhounds, and over 13 million other dogs, dying every year for the want of a home, one would have to be either incredibly naive or thoughtless to even consider bringing another Greyhound litter into the world. Don't forget that 30 percent of the dogs that wind up in shelters are purebred. No matter how beautiful or talented or good-natured your dog is, there are hundreds more just as good, or even better. So don't think that by breeding your dog you will be creating more "perfect" specimens. Other perfect specimens of all kinds already exist, and they are dying by the millions!

As for breeding ex-racers to other breeds of dogs, or to AKC Greyhounds, forget that too. The bottom line with *all* breeding is that there are already more dogs (and cats) in the world than there are homes for them. Even if you think you will find good homes for all of the puppies you create, what about the puppies' puppies? And their puppies? And what about the homes you have "taken up" because you chose to breed your dog? You can be sure that other deserving dogs already alive will now die because there is no room for them.

And, if you think that your dog will never be bred because you are just too careful, bear in mind that most mixed-breed dogs are the result of accidental matings. The sexual urge is very strong when a female is in heat and a male is on her trail. Dogs have been known to move heaven and earth to get at the object of their affection. It only takes a moment's inattention from you and it could be too late.

Health Advantages

The health advantages to spaying and neutering are considerable. Male dogs that have not been neutered are prone to testicular cancer in their older years as well as prostate trouble. Uterine cancer and mammary tumors are common in unspayed females, as is pyrometra, an infection of the uterus than can be fatal if not treated promptly. I have been asked why these diseases do not kill wild or feral dogs, and the answer is that in some cases they do. However, because wild and feral dogs are sexually and reproductively active, the various organs are kept in good shape. By contrast, a domestic, unneutered male dog that is constantly stimulated by the odor of females in heat, but who never has the chance to breed, can develop chronic inflammations. Likewise, unspayed females who regularly go into heat but are never bred are also prone to problems. It really is more humane, from many standpoints, to spay and neuter.

GROOMING

In general, Greyhounds are very clean and do not need a tremendous amount of care. That does not mean, however, that they should only be bathed once a year whether they need it or not. Grooming allows you to spend quality time with your dog, increases the bond between you and gives you the opportunity to head off potential health problems before they become serious.

If your dog is prone to fleas, a nontoxic flea bath once every ten days should be enough. More washing than that will dry out his coat and skin. (See Chapter Six for specific recommendations concerning flea prevention.) Otherwise, a bath every six to eight weeks helps remove dead hair and keeps him smelling fresh. Always use a shampoo made specifically for dogs. Human shampoo will dry out a dog's skin even with only one washing because the pH balance of dog skin is different from ours.

The Best Way to Bathe Your Dog

Do not bathe your dog in cold water. Even on the hottest summer day, a Greyhound can become deeply chilled by the icy water of a garden hose. The preferred method is to bathe your dog in a bathtub. You may want to have someone hold him, or you can simply tie his leash to the water faucets so that he can stand comfortably but cannot escape. Be sure to provide a nonslip surface on the bottom of the tub.

Ideally you'll have a device for the faucet that acts as a shower or spray. If you don't have one, then fill a plastic bowl (not glass, please) with warm water. Plug the dog's ears with cotton and wet him thoroughly. Next, shampoo, taking care to avoid the eyes and mouth. Rinse thoroughly (shampoo residue can cause flaking skin), repeat as necessary, and you're done. Most Greyhounds will stand quietly for all of this even if they aren't crazy about it! Always dry your dog completely, and, in cold weather, keep him out of drafts and do not allow him outside for several hours after the bath.

While you are bathing him, check his ears for dirt and ticks. If you see dirt, wipe it out with a cotton ball, not a cotton swab. If the dirt has a foul odor or is very thick, he may have an ear infection, so see your veterinarian. Check toenail length at bath time, too.

Finally, brush the coat daily with a flat rubber or sisal glove (called, appropriately enough, a hound glove) or a fine-tooth comb. Most Greyhounds love being brushed and practically purr with delight. You might try a little muscle massage at the same time. You'll soon discover that grooming will become the highlight of the day for both of you.

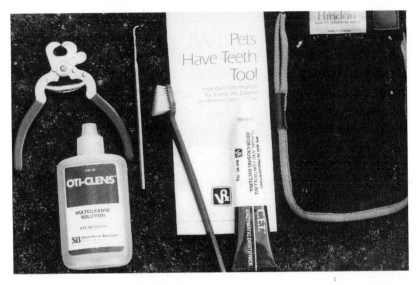

Some items for grooming (clockwise from bottom left): ear cleaning solution, toenail trimmers, tooth scaler, canine toothbrush and toothpaste, and grooming glove.

DENTAL CARE

Most dogs that are just off the track have terrible-looking teeth covered with tartar. More than one veterinarian has looked skeptical when told that a certain dog was only two or three when what he or she saw looked more like the mouth of a ten-year-old. The reason is that racing dogs have a totally soft diet and so the tartar builds quickly. Also, many gnaw on their crates out of boredom and wear their teeth down.

Get your dog's teeth cleaned regularly by a veterinarian to prevent tooth loss and gum infection. This can be done initially while the dog is being spayed or neutered, so he has to be anesthetized only once. To maintain clean teeth, brush your dog's teeth weekly with special dog toothpaste.

Your veterinarian will have it available as do pet supply catalogues. Also, hard dog biscuits, sterilized cow hooves and rawhide strips help keep dogs' teeth clean, and they really love it. Many people also give their dogs raw carrots to gnaw on. That way the dogs clean their teeth, massage their gums and get their vitamins all at once!

If you want to get really adventurous, you can try scaling your dog's teeth yourself. Dental tools are available in many pet supply stores. Start at the gum line and gently move the tool back and forth, gradually working your way toward the tip of the tooth. It takes patience, both on the part of the person *and* the dog, but it can avoid a yearly trip to the veterinarian's office for dentistry.

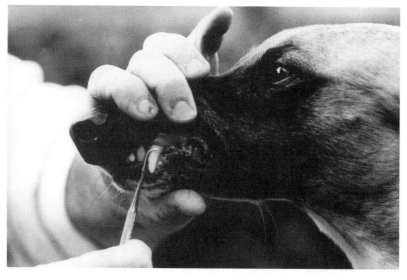

Sophie's teeth are scaled to remove tartar.

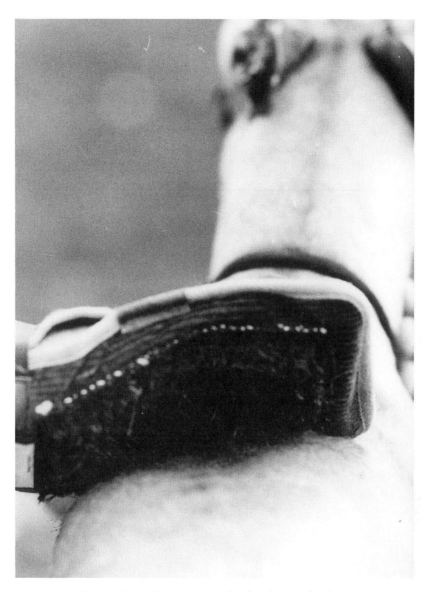

Grooming the coat with the hound glove.

Greyhounds love to be stroked.

ASSISTING THE OLDER DOG

A word about the older Greyhound. As with people, a dog's senses become weaker as he ages. Age comes on so gradually that many owners fail to notice that their old friend is not responding the way he used to. Impaired sight or hearing loss puts a dog at a disadvantage. It does not, however, have to mean the end.

As I write this, I have two canine senior citizens living with me—King, the Greyhound, who is thirteen and a half, and Jasper, the rescued Afghan Hound, who is approximately fifteen. King's eyesight is greatly diminished by cataracts and damaged rods in his eyes. He has compensated by relying more and more on his sense of smell. I have assisted him by keeping the furniture in the same place, leaving a night light on for him and by always lighting the stairwell

The old guard, Jasper (foreground) and King.

for him when he is going up or down. Jasper no longer has perfect bladder control, so I removed the carpeting in the living room and refinished the wood floor so that when it is necessary, I can mop up without a problem. His dog bed has a plastic-covered foam pad inside with a fleece cover outside that can be removed easily for washing.

Old age for a dog does not have to mean misery either for you or for him. When you reflect on all the pleasure dogs bring you during the course of their life, I'm sure you'll agree that they are worth making a few modifications for so that they can maintain their dignity and you can continue to be enriched by their company.

CHAPTER

6

INSECTICIDES
AND
ANESTHESIA

/ / / / / / / / / / / /

As you've probably already realized, Greyhounds are very sensitive creatures. What you may not know, however, is that this sensitivity also extends to their reactions to certain drugs and chemicals. The information in this chapter will help you provide safe relief for your dog from such pests as fleas as well as enable you to discuss with your veterinarian the anesthesia best suited for Greyhounds should the need arise.

FLEA COLLARS

In our attempt to rid our pets from fleas, we Americans have exposed ourselves, and our animals, to an assortment of toxic chemicals. Take, for example, seemingly innocuous flea collars. They are sold everywhere, and one could almost be lulled into thinking that they are both safe and effective. In fact they are neither. Flea collars have their origins in nerve gas chemical warfare and they work by permeating the skin of your animal's neck and, eventually, paralyzing and killing the flea that bites the skin. They should *never* encircle the neck of a Greyhound nor, in my opinion, any other animal.

Some of the chemicals commonly found in flea collars can, in a Greyhound and other sensitive and/or allergic animals, cause nausea, convulsions and even death.

An added hazard is that we dispose of over *50 million* of these collars every year, which means that they add to the already growing toxic waste problem we face in this country.

In general I believe we, as a culture, have become far too casual in our use of toxic chemicals. One look at the state of our air and water will confirm that. So, too, have we become too casual about the chemicals we put on our pets. As it turns out, because of the way their bodies metabolize these substances, Greyhounds are extremely sensitive to many pesticides, so there is no margin for error.

Similarly, the chemical compounds found in various flea shampoos, dips and sprays can be equally deadly.

INSECTICIDES

Most insecticides can be grouped into one of three families: the organophosphates, the carbamates and the pyrethrins. Neither the first nor the second should ever be considered for use on Greyhounds.

Organophosphates

Some examples of organophosphates are malathion, diazinon and chlorpyrifos (sold as Dursban), all of which are used in various potent flea killers. As with flea collars, I don't believe any animal (or human) should be exposed to them, but especially not Greyhounds. A recent study conducted at the University of Washington showed that even a single episode of poisoning worthy of treatment could lead to "a persistent decline in neuropsychological performance."

Carbamates

The next group, carbamates, include carbaryl (sold as Sevin) as well as other carbamate compounds. These, too, hold the potential for a bad reaction, either in the short term with immediate symptoms (such as profuse salivating, labored breathing, vomiting, etc.) or in the long term (nervous system damage or cancer).

Pyrethrins

Pyrethrins are the least toxic of the three and are a natural substance derived from the chrysanthemum flower. Pyrethroids (such as permethrin, allethrin and resmethrin) are manmade equivalents. They are strong enough to kill most fleas but have a very low toxicity level for mammals. It is very popular to mix pyrethrins with piperonyl butoxide. This is a synergist that, although toxic, can be used sparingly (combined with pyrethrins) if an infestation is especially severe.

Also to be avoided are chemicals (cythiolate, propoxur and fenthion) that are applied monthly to the length of the dog's spine or in a spot on the base of the neck (sold as

Rabon, Baygon, ProSpot, Ex-Spot, etc.). They are much too strong for a Greyhound, and you are risking damage or, possibly, death. In general, if a product says "safe for puppies and kittens" it will be safe for a Greyhound.

NATURAL FLEA CONTROL

I know, however, how maddening an infestation of fleas can be and so here are some effective, nontoxic ways to deal with the problem.

First of all, it is important to treat your home and not just the dog. Fleas come from the environment and so you must eliminate them there. Vacuum daily and throw away the vacuum bag. Also, wash the dog's bedding frequently. Heat also kills fleas, so you can toss their pillows in a hot dryer.

One of the 2,237 species of fleas.

Insect Growth Regulator

A relatively new product, which is called an insect growth regulator (IGR), eliminates fleas by preventing them from reproducing. Given that two adult fleas can produce over one million offspring in a year, it is essential that their reproductive cycle be broken. Generally the products, which go by the trade names of Precor and Torus, are sprayed all over the house and in the animal's sleeping areas. One warning: sometimes companies combine IGR's with toxic chemicals. Make sure what you buy (or what you have applied by an exterminator) is in its pure form.

Herbal Preparations

The only completely safe products to apply directly to your Greyhound's skin are herbal formulas, which vary in effectiveness, and pyrethrins. Most herbs simply drive fleas away but don't kill them. Pyrethrins work by literally choking fleas to death. Pyrethrin formulas are found in powders and shampoos, but read the label carefully and avoid toxic additives.

Dietary Additives

Some people use dietary means to control fleas. One woman I know dusts her dogs with brewer's yeast weekly and adds it to the animals' food. Many people report success with garlic capsules. Still others swear by the addition of vitamins. I have tried all of the above with little success. They do serve, however, to bolster your dog's immune system, so, if for no other reason, they may be worth a try.

The Flea Comb

There is one sure-fire way to keep fleas (and ticks) from your Greyhound that is totally nontoxic. It's by using a flea comb, and while it is anything but a high-tech device, it really works! I comb my dogs (and cats) daily and find that although it is a bit time-consuming, it is a way to groom your animal safely and spend some time with him.

The best way to use a flea comb is to first get set up with two bowls of water: one soapy and warm, the other clear and warm. Then place your pet right next to the soapy water bowl. Now comb through once (with the hair, not against it), and you'll see fleas (if there are any) and flea dirt trapped between the fine teeth of the comb. Immediately dip the comb in the soapy water. The dirt will fall off and the fleas will drown as the soap clogs their lungs. Make sure the comb is flea-free, then rinse in clear water before you make the next pass through the animal's fur. You'll see that the dog will come to enjoy the combing both for the relief it brings and for the time you're spending with him.

DEWORMERS

Ridding your Greyhound of internal parasites (worms) is another area in which you must be careful. Droncit is the drug of choice for tapeworm (a by-product of having fleas). Use Droncit in tablet form not injection. Not only are tablets cheaper, but they minimize the possibility of a painful injection. Panacur (also called Safeguard) is best for hookworm, roundworm and whipworm. Task is definitely *not* recommended for use against worms in Greyhounds, as it has an organophosphate base. As you now know, Greyhounds are extremely sensitive to this substance, and you could very well create more problems than you would solve. Be sure to make your veterinarian aware of this if he is not already.

ANESTHESIA AND THE GREYHOUND

How they respond to anesthesia is another way in which Greyhounds (and other sighthounds) are different from other breeds of dogs. If you think your veterinarian may not be familiar with these differences, you might want to lend him this book so he can read the next section for up-to-date information on the subject.

One reason why Greyhounds react as they do to drugs is that their liver metabolizes them more slowly. Another factor is the breed's low percentage of body fat proportionate to its size. Greyhounds have, on the average, 16 percent bodyweight of fat as compared with 35 percent bodyweight of fat in mixed breed dogs of similar weight. The level of some drugs in a dog's system falls by going into its fat. The less fat, the longer it takes for the blood level to fall.

Certain forms of anesthesia are safer than others for Greyhounds. Bear in mind that all anesthesia, whether for dogs or humans, carries some risk. Never avoid necessary surgery because of this risk, but do select a veterinarian who will talk with you and choose the safest type of anesthesia and administer it in the safest way. (Also, when practical, combine procedures such as spaying or neutering with a teeth cleaning. That way a dog only has to be anesthetized once.)

Dr. Alan Klide, associate professor of veterinary anesthesia at the University of Pennsylvania School of Veterinary Medicine, has this to say about anesthesia for Greyhounds: "It is common practice to give a drug to calm dogs before anesthesia is begun and also to give them one to make them dry and prevent the heart from slowing. If

Greyhounds being treated by early "veterinarians" in a fifteenth-century French print.

Greyhounds are given a higher dose of narcotic, then they will need less thiobarbiturate. There are many narcotics, but the one that is most useful and safe, in dogs, is called oxymorphone. Glycopyrrolate, one of two drugs used to dry secretions, allows the dogs to wake up sooner than if the other drug, atropine, is used."

Thiobarbiturates
Further, Dr. Klide suggests that "This whole problem can be avoided by not using a thiobarbiturate. There are other drugs

which can be injected to begin anesthesia. One called methohexital is commonly used by veterinarians to anesthetize Greyhounds. There are two relatively new intravenous anesthetics which look promising for anesthetizing Greyhounds, and these are propofol and ctomidate.

"There are several inhaled anesthetics which are used in veterinary and human anesthesia. In general, halothane is well tolerated in normal individuals. A newer anesthetic which may be useful in some circumstances is isoflurane."

All of the Greyhounds adopted through Make Peace With Animals are spayed or neutered before entering their new homes. The ones anesthetized with isoflurane seem to "come around" much more quickly.

Malignant Hyperthermia

Greyhounds can experience a further reaction to anesthesia. Dr. Klide explains:

"There is a disease of humans and some animals which is rare, but very severe. It has been reported in Greyhounds. It is called malignant hyperthermia. When the individual with this condition is stressed or anesthetized with certain anesthetics, including all the available inhaled ones, they get very hot, may get stiff and will probably die unless they are given a drug called dantrolene. If a dog or its relatives has such a condition in its history, it should be given dantrolene before, during and for a few days after it is anesthetized.

"When other drugs such as sedatives or tranquilizers need to be given to Greyhounds, if possible, a low dose should be tried first."

Ways to Speed Recovery

To discourage a prolonged recovery in a Greyhound, Dr. Klide notes the following:

- "Intravenous fluids may have to be limited because of heart disease.

- Keep the dog warm; cold prolongs the depth and duration of anesthesia.

- Provide mechanical ventilation if necessary.

- Administer oxygen if necessary.

- Turn the dog periodically to try to prevent the occurrence of pneumonia.

- Measure blood sugar and make normal if not normal."

LAWN CHEMICALS AND CANINE CANCER

One final piece of advice pertains to the use of herbicides on your lawn. There was a time when people (and companies) would use whatever chemicals were needed to rid a lawn of weeds and promote green grass. Not so anymore.

A commonly used weed-killing chemical compound called 2, 4-D has been linked to cancer in dogs. In fact, dogs that walk on treated lawns are twice as likely to develop lymphatic cancer. And, if the lawn is treated four or more times a year, a dog's risk of developing cancer doubles.

Are your dogs safe from the hazards of herbicides?

Studies are now underway to see what health hazards are posed to humans. So, if you value your dog's health (and possibly your own), avoid the use of herbicides on your lawn.

CHAPTER
7
TRAINING

////////////

When you adopt a retired racing Greyhound, you are getting a dog that is already extensively trained. The problem is that some of the training is irrelevant to his new life as a companion. As such, there are some new tricks that you must teach these "old" dogs as well as some old tricks that you must help them to forget.

It is uncanny how most Greyhounds seem to be right at home even though they've never before been in a house. I've concocted a rather elaborate legend to explain this.

Long ago, in a racing kennel far away, a Greyhound went home for the night with his trainer. He was a very intelligent and very observant Greyhound, because when he went back to the kennel the next day he was able to recount to his fellow racers every detail of what it was like to spend the night in a house. Because he was a Greyhound who was exceptionally fond of pleasure, he gave special attention to details of soft places to sleep and where the food was kept.

Since the other Greyhounds had little to occupy their minds with other than thoughts of chasing the lure, they took great delight in these tales of home life. And so, by oral

*Ajax carries his pillow everywhere and uses it for—
what else?—a head rest!*

tradition, the story spread. Mother Greyhounds told the tale to their young pups. Old male Greyhounds told it to young males. Over the years the details of what it was like to live in a house spread to every racing kennel in the land. And that is why Greyhounds behave as if they've waited all their lives for the experience of living with you—because they have!

Unfortunately, over the years some of the story became exaggerated (that Greyhounds are to be fed steak upon request) while other parts were left out entirely (like the fact that not everyone wants a dog on the sofa). So now it is up to you to set the record straight and establish the rules of the house.

HOUSEBREAKING

One rule that everyone will agree on is that the dog must be housebroken. The reason for it is obvious. What is not so obvious to some people is how to accomplish it.

You have a leg up (no pun intended) on the process by virtue of the fact that racing dogs have already been crate trained. In the kennels Greyhounds are housed in large crates (cages) and are let out four times a day to exercise and relieve themselves. For most dogs it does not take a very big leap of the imagination to see your entire house as a crate.

The first thing you need to do is keep your dog on a schedule. As much as possible, try to adapt yours to his. In other words, if you usually get up at nine in the morning but you know the dog is used to waking at seven, get up earlier at first, then gradually change the dog's sleeping patterns.

Take the Dog Out Often

The basics of housebreaking apply to racing Greyhounds just like any other breed. Walk the dog first thing in the morning, after both meals, midday if possible, and before bed. Keep an eye on the dog in between, too. If he seems restless and begins pacing, he may need to go out. Bear in mind that the dog may be a little uneasy in his new surroundings, and this, combined with new food and water, may affect his bowels and bladder.

Use the Crate

In Chapter Three I talked about the importance of crates in easing the transition from kennel to home. Most of what was said there concerned preventing the dog from hurting himself or becoming destructive in the home. Yet crates are useful tools for housebreaking, too.

Since racing Greyhounds are crate trained, you can prevent "accidents" in the house by putting the dog in a crate. They have been trained not to soil their crates, and rare indeed is the Greyhound that will.

If you take your dog out four or five times a day, if you keep an eye on him the rest of the time and if the dog sleeps in the crate at night, there is little room for error.

There are exceptions, of course.

I have found that a few modest Greyhounds are uncomfortable relieving themselves while someone is holding them on a leash. You can walk them for miles, but if they know you're there watching, they won't do their "business." Later, this type of dog, in desperation, usually finds a remote corner of the house to relieve himself. What should you do? The answer is simple: if you have a fenced yard, let him run loose. But what if you don't? Three choices: find a fenced area, fence in a small area yourself or require the dog to get used to being on lead. The second or third choices are the ones you will eventually make, because it certainly isn't very convenient to travel to someone else's fenced yard four times a day just so your dog can have some privacy!

BEHAVIORAL "ACCIDENTS"

As to another perplexing housebreaking problem, some "accidents" aren't accidents. The dog is quite intentionally marking his (or her) territory. For this I recommend scolding the dog firmly but gently and putting him in the crate. You must be consistent and react the same way every time. Don't scream. Greyhounds are far too sensitive for that. And, of course, never ever strike them. A serious tone of voice coupled with the crate is all you need to address the problem.

HEALTH PROBLEMS

Don't overlook the possibility that your dog may have developed a health problem. Diarrhea or persistent urinating in the house may be the sign that something is physically wrong. Have your dog checked by a veterinarian, especially if he was housebroken then suddenly isn't.

If for some reason you choose not to use a crate, keep your dog confined to one room—preferably the kitchen—and spread newspaper on the floor. Bathrooms tend to be too small and can cause a dog to feel claustrophobic and panicky, while basements are generally dark and give the dog the feeling of being shut off from the rest of the house. Never put your ex-racer in a garage! Remember, the idea is to acclimate your dog to become a part of the family. Garages are for cars, not for your companions.

OBEDIENCE TRAINING

I recommend a basic obedience course to everyone who adopts an ex-racer. A well-trained dog is a real asset. Not only is he easier to live with, but also he has a very clear idea of his boundaries and becomes comfortable and secure knowing that when he does what you want, you are happy with him. Most dogs, and especially Greyhounds, are eager to please.

A dog's training could also save his life. A dog that is out of control rarely remains with the same family who originally adopted him. Take a visit to any animal shelter and you will see many dogs, purebreds and mixed breeds alike, that never had the benefit of basic training. Sadly, most of them will be euthanized because when people are looking to adopt a dog, the trained ones are the first to be chosen. Should your dog ever have to be readopted, good training is an investment in his future. How many people do you know who would be interested in adopting an older dog that chews shoes, jumps up on people and pulls on the leash?

Choosing a Good Trainer

There is no special requirement for a basic obedience course other that it be accomplished humanely. Greyhounds are extremely sensitive, and if the course instructor believes in shouting, instilling fear, using choke collars with metal prongs or, worst of all, electric shocks, don't walk away, run! I have seen Greyhounds who have endured cruel training and they have never recovered. Their spirit was broken and they developed many neurotic habits as a result.

You should also decline to participate in a program if the teachers recommend leaving the dog behind so they can train him alone. A wonderful bond is established between you and your dog when you take an obedience course together. Actually, you are both being trained—you are being trained as the pack leader and the dog is being trained to look to you for guidance. By leaving the job to someone else, there will always be a missing link. Besides, who knows what kind of training will take place after you've gone home?

Getting the Greyhound to Sit

Frequently I am asked, "Can Greyhounds sit?" My answer is "Yes, but most of them prefer not to." It isn't painful for them but I get the distinct impression that it is uncomfortable. Usually you'll find a Greyhound in one of three poses: standing, crouching (with forelegs extended, chest resting on the floor) or lying on his side. There's nothing wrong with any of these postures except that they take up a bit of room. If you insist that the dog be taught to sit, train him the same way you'd train any other dog. Gently pull up on his collar while pushing down on his rump. He may not get it at first, but with practice he will. By the way, one myth that has been circulating is that racing Greyhounds are trained *not* to sit so they will leave the starting box quicker. This is not true. Racing dogs are naturally eager to take off and sitting is the last thing on their minds.

TOOLS OF THE TRADE

The Muzzle

All racing dogs are transported with muzzles. In the Introduction, I explained that it is not because Greyhounds are vicious, but, rather, because all dogs are more prone to aggression when they are under stress, be it the stress of chasing a lure or of traveling in close quarters.

When you adopt an ex-racer, the muzzle is part of his "dowry." It will become an essential part of training him when he first meets your other pets.

Most Greyhounds are excellent with small dogs and cats. A few aren't. You don't want to find out the hard way in which category he belongs. Exercise caution. Just because the dogs is wonderful and affectionate with you, doesn't mean he wouldn't chase, and kill, a cat. And just because he gets along with dogs his own size doesn't mean he would be able to resist catching your toy dog.

The Correct Collar

When walking your dog on a leash, always use a choke collar. The reason for this is simple: the head of a Greyhound is very narrow and a regular collar would have to be kept on so tight that it would choke the dog continually. At the racetrack leashes are rarely used; the person leading the dog uses the dog's collar as a handle. That way the dog cannot escape. But in life on the outside it is not practical to hold your dog by the collar.

A choke collar will stay slack until the moment it is needed, and only then will it tighten up. You would be amazed at the ease with which a regular collar can slip right over a Greyhound's ears. Before you know it, the dog is gone and you are left holding an empty collar. Some Greyhounds are quite expert at backing out of their collars, too. Regular collars are fine for wear around the house and

Racing muzzles, made of molded plastic, are used only during a race.

to hold I.D. and rabies tags, but some sort of a restraining collar is essential for use on the street. Many people I know keep a choker and leash permanently attached and slip it on the dog as they go out and slip it off when they come in. The people who do this keep a regular collar (with I.D. tags) on at all times, just in case the dog ever dashes out the door. The choker is used only for walks. There is always the possibility, albeit remote, that a choke collar could get caught on something and actually choke the dog when you aren't around, so it's best to reserve their use for the leash only.

When the temperature dips below 32 degrees, Greyhounds need coats.

"Humane" Choke Collars

Of the various choke collars on the market, the one I recommend, and indeed the one I give out with each adoption, has a slightly different construction than the traditional choker. It consists of two flat nylon circles, a smaller one intertwined with the larger. When the choke action is needed, it restrains the dog firmly and securely yet never pinches the throat or gags the dog. This type of collar is known generically as either a martingale collar or as a humane choker. As far as I'm concerned, no Greyhound should be without one.

If you choose to use a standard choke collar, make it a flat or rounded nylon one rather than a chain choker. Greyhound skin is too sensitive for the metal ones.

The collar no Greyhound should be without. Tracey models the humane choker.

Sophie shows off a slip-lead for quick release in coursing.

Holding the Leash Properly

While we are on the subject of collars, let me say a few words about leashes. Many people do not hold a leash correctly. There is a reason why there is a loop at one end of the leash, and that is so you can put your hand through it. Only once the loop is over your hand and is resting around the outside of your wrist do you take hold of the leash. Holding the leash correctly prevents it from ever slipping out of your hand.

As for what type of leash to get, I recommend either four-or six-foot lengths. If your dog is a chewer, try a metal chain leash. Otherwise nylon or leather will do nicely. There is no particular advantage to the extendable/retractable leash, but the disadvantages are that the dog can get farther away from you, can easily get tangled up around you or something else and in general provides less control.

Using a Harness

If you choose to use a harness rather than a collar and leash, fine. A harness does provide good control, but it is somewhat of a nuisance to put on and take off. It should, of course, be taken off when not needed, as it can chafe and irritate a dog's skin. Don't forget to keep the appropriate I.D. tags, licenses, etc., attached to a collar. You never want your dog to be without identification, even at home.

Just because you choose to use a harness doesn't mean you can tie the dog in the yard either on a runner or to a stake. With a dog capable of reaching high speeds in a short period of time, even the snapping back of a harness when the dog reaches the end of his tether could injure him severely.

Remember, walk a Greyhound on a leash or release him in a completely fenced area *only*.

This is a chapter that you may want to read over a few times. The information in it comes from personal experiences I have had with these wonderful dogs. If you can learn from some of the mistakes that others have made, then perhaps those mistakes were not in vain. And, once you and your dog have reached an understanding with each other about the way things are, you will have the best companion in the world.

MEETING OTHER DOGS

To introduce your new Greyhound to dogs his own size (or any size down to about twenty pounds), let them first sniff each other with a closed door between them. Dogs can tell a lot about each other from their scent. Let them have plenty of time to get the full doggy bouquet, then, with both the Greyhound and your old dog on leashes, let them meet. A lot more sniffing will occur. If you see either dog's hackles rise, move them apart. It is only one Greyhound in a million that will start a fight with another dog, so if either is the instigator, it will probably be your old dog. Gradually they will establish which one is dominant, and they will probably become best friends.

Meeting Very Small Dogs and Cats

If you have small dogs or cats, bring your Greyhound into the house on a leash and *wearing his muzzle*. This is essential because, as you know by now, Greyhounds are terribly fast. Should they pull the leash away from you, at least you'll have the insurance of a muzzle. I once heard of a couple who adopted out Greyhounds advise new owners not to use the muzzle on the theory that they would be giving the dog a mixed message. They incorrectly thought that by using the muzzle you would be indicating to the dog that it was time to race. Nothing could be further from the truth. The racing muzzles are of a completely different construction from the type you will get, which are used only when the dogs travel or are turned out together. Believe me, the racers know the difference!

I remember when I adopted my original Greyhound, King, I told the person from whom I took him that if he went

A classic sighthound restraining collar.

after my cats I would have to return him. As it turned out, he was terrified of the cats and trembled and cried during the first month he was with them. Needless to say, we had no trouble. My second Greyhound, Ajax, was totally un-afraid and barely acknowledged the cats' existence. No trou-ble there, either.

Signs of trouble are when the dog actively lunges at the small pets, barks or growls, or is just too interested. A certain degree of interest is normal. They are sighthounds, after all, and they respond to visual stimuli. But "too much interest" is when they literally can't take their eyes off the pet, they begin to crouch down as if to spring forward or they whine in the direction of where they last saw the pet. Should you see any of these signs, keep the muzzle on and keep the dog on a leash, and under no circumstances should you leave them alone together.

TRAINING

One woman who adopted a female Greyhound from me had a unique way of introducing Stacy to her three cats. She had a life-size, and very life-like, sculpture of a cat in her living room. As soon as Stacy spied it, she was very curious. While keeping her leashed (no need for a muzzle), the owner slowly let Stacy examine the sculpture. After a few "meetings," she let Stacy encounter the real thing (with a muzzle and leash, of course). There were no problems, and we suspect that meeting the fake cat in advance allowed Stacy to get used to a small creature in a relaxed way. I've not tried this myself, but it sounds logical and it worked for Stacy.

To correct a dog that may see these small pets as prey, use a choke collar, and whenever they attempt to lunge, jerk the collar and firmly say "No." Eventually you will "deprogram" all but the most intractable from their racing training. If a dog does not respond to your corrections within a few days, think about exchanging him for a dog that does not have the chasing urge so deeply ingrained. For some dogs, no amount of correcting will work, and you don't want a tragedy on your hands. By the way, even though most dogs eventually will respect the small pets in the house, outside may be a different story. The house, after all, is your domain, but as far as they are concerned, outside is up for grabs. You'll have to teach them otherwise, the same way you taught them inside.

Don't be alarmed by the information you've just read in this section. Most Greyhounds are just fine with small pets. And even the ones who aren't initially can usually be trained into complying. I say "usually," because I believe there are a very few for whom the racing instinct is just too strong. There are extreme ways to get a dog to stop chasing, but I prefer taking the dog back and placing it in another home where there will be no temptation. I care for cats and small dogs too much to jeopardize their lives, and I respect the

Greyhounds too much to put them through strenuous and unkind training.

RETRIEVING A LOST GREYHOUND

You may recall that in the first chapter I discussed the hazards of intentionally letting an ex-racer run off-lead. There is always the chance, though, that it will happen unintentionally. Of course we can't control everything, but it is prudent to be as careful as possible.

If you experience the misfortune of having a Greyhound run away from you or your yard, there is one way of getting him back that is sometimes more effective than simply calling him. It involves using a device intended for hunting that simulates the sound of an animal in distress. It is usually referred to as a squawker. A similar device is also used at the track when, at the finish line, one of the dogs starts heading in the wrong direction. The sound of the squawker gets his attention there, and it may do the same in your neighborhood. Squawkers are available at hunting supply stores as well as through mail-order catalogs.

"Invisible" Fencing

Frequently I am asked about fencing that is operated by a radio signal. If a dog crosses a predetermined boundary, a slight shock is delivered to his neck through a special collar. To put it simply, I don't like the system, and here's why.

I feel that racing Greyhounds have had quite enough negative reinforcement training to last them a lifetime. A shock to the neck, no matter how slight, would certainly be too much of a shock to the system for some of the more sensitive Greyhounds that I've met. Besides, I had a salesman come to my property once, and I asked to feel the intensity of the shock collar. I put it against my leg (which I believe is less sensitive than a Greyhound's neck) and found it to be quite irritating. While not exactly painful, it was definitely startling and uncomfortable. I sent the man packing.

Another reason is that while these fences supposedly keep dogs in (and even that is up for debate—I once knew a Whippet named Wicket who would run through, shock or not), they don't keep other dogs, animals or people out. So, a vicious neighborhood dog could come into your "protected" yard and attack your Greyhound. A rabid raccoon could do likewise. And, perhaps worst of all, a person could walk in and steal your Greyhound.

Finally, the speed with which Greyhounds run means that the length of time they are exposed to the correcting shock of the collar is very short—so short that it may not make a difference to them. Like little Wicket, they'll run through anyway.

HOME ALONE, YES—IN THE YARD ALONE, NO

Never leave your dog outside in the yard while you are not at home. Let me explain why.

A dog that may be perfectly calm in the yard as long as he knows you are in the house may go into a panic if he sees you drive away. Fear is a powerful emotion, and if the dog thinks he is somehow being abandoned, he is going to do everything possible to get to you. Everything may include jumping the fence, digging beneath it or even managing to unlatch the gate. Believe me, it has happened.

Another potential hazard in leaving a dog unattended in a fenced yard is that another animal may get in. A fight, started either by your dog, who is protecting his territory, or by the intruder, may ensue. Who will be there to break it up?

It's not only animals that can get into your yard. People can, too. It could be someone as innocuous as the meter reader, who doesn't latch the gate properly when he leaves, or it could be someone who steals dogs from unattended yards. There are such people who make their living by stealing dogs for resale to research laboratories.

Finally there is the weather to consider. Greyhounds have poor tolerance for both heat and cold. Haven't you noticed that, on some days, you leave for work and it is bright and sunny when, out of nowhere, the clouds move in. Before you know it, the temperature has dropped twenty degrees and you wish you'd taken a sweater with you. Think of the Greyhound with his thin skin and virtually no body fat. With neither fur nor fat for protection, Greyhounds are strictly indoor dogs.

FENCING BASICS

The vast majority of Greyhounds are not jumpers, so the height of the fence can be as low as five feet, but never any lower. Remember, though, that the fence must be higher if it is erected on a hillside. The downward slope could give the dog an added height advantage. You will also be pleased to know that most are not diggers. In all of my adoptions, I've placed only four that were climbers, so for them, a chain link fence was out. Stockade or some sort of smooth wood was the only type that they could not climb.

Safe, Inexpensive Fencing

I am often asked what is the best type of fencing for ex-racers. Ideally, it should be smooth wood, 6 feet in height. You can get by with a foot less, however.

If money is a consideration, you may want to erect the type of fence I chose. It is made of heavy wire, comes in fifty-foot rolls, and is coated with a dark green vinyl. You need to buy metal stake-type fence posts that can be driven into the ground with a hammer (another advantage). The wire is simply unrolled, stretched across your yard and attached to the little hooks protruding from the stakes. It was so easy even I could do it! Remember to get at least the 5-foot height with six-foot posts. (Note: Five-foot fencing should be the minimum. The posts are one foot taller as one foot is hammered into the ground. Top of posts should be even with top of fence.) I don't think it comes any higher, but it does come lower, and a Greyhound could practically walk over that. Always check to make sure your fence gates are closed; don't assume they are simply because they were yesterday. Likewise, check your fencing from time to time to be sure it's in good condition. I know from experience that things can happen even to the best fencing.

CHAPTER

8

HAVING

FUN

////////////

The ways in which you can have fun with your ex-racer are limited only by your imagination. In fact, there are certain things you can do with Greyhounds that you can't do with any other breed of dog.

ARTIFICIAL LURE COURSING

Take, for example, artificial lure coursing. A plastic bag (a rag or a pelt) is dragged across a field by a motorized cord on a predetermined course. It is virtually unknown outside sighthound circles, and the reason is that the sport depends on the dog's ability to see the artificial lure and to take off after it. As we know, Greyhounds are sighthounds—they hunt by sight rather than by scent as do most other dogs. A Bloodhound would be distinctly nonplussed at the sight of a white plastic bag being dragged across a field. In fact, when he could no longer see the bag, it would lose what little interest it held initially.

Not so with sighthounds. To them, a white plastic bag whipping across a field is enough to make them quiver in anticipation. It stirs up thousands of years of genetics (plus whatever training your racer had at the track) and is a sport made to order. Coursing as a sport grew out of the sighthounds' method of hunting. Not only do they hunt by sight, but they are also used to working as a team with others of their kind. Coursing makes use of both skills.

The Requirements

Specifically, the way a lure coursing trial works is this:

All events are held under the auspices of the American Sighthound Field Association (ASFA). Dogs that are allowed to compete (the ten sighthound breeds recognized by the AKC) must be registered with the American Kennel Club or the National Greyhound Association. Since you have a former racer, the latter applies. However, in certain circumstances you may not be able to get a copy of your dog's NGA volume and certificate number. If that is so, you can apply to the AKC for an Indefinite Listing Privilege (ILP) number. Call and ask them to send you an application. You must include several photos of your Greyhound so they can determine that he is the real thing. Several weeks later you will receive an ILP number in the mail, and that is what you will use to enter your dog in a competition.

Coursing events are held on an open field far from traffic and other hazards of civilization. All dogs must be kept on a leash or crated unless they are competing. On the day of the event, each hound that has been entered to participate must be present for roll call. At that time, all the hounds are checked for lameness and, in the case of bitches, to see if they are in heat. If either condition is present, the hound is excused and the entry fee is returned. Dogs that have dew

119

claws, and almost all racers do, must have them taped to their legs so that they do not become tangled in the cord that pulls the lure.

Next, a random drawing takes place to determine the order in which the breeds compete. Only dogs of the same breed compete with each other (i.e., Greyhounds with Greyhounds, Borzois with Borzois, etc.) and are run in groups of three (trios). If necessary, two dogs run together. After the preliminary course, during which each dog will have run twice and earned a certain number of points, another random draw is conducted to determine the order of breeds for the final courses. Dogs that have run together the first time around are not necessarily paired during the finals.

The Judging

After the finals, the dogs with the highest scores compete with each other, and the winner of that course is designated Best of Breed. All dogs are ultimately working toward the title of Lure Courser of Merit, but that requires many points and many competitions. The main thing is to have fun and to watch your dog enjoy himself.

Lure coursing is an especially exciting sport because the dogs are judged by more than one criterion. A dog can get up to 100 points from each course, and the breakdown of maximum points per category is as follows:

Enthusiasm. . . . . . . .15 points
Follow . . . . .15 points
Speed. . . . . .25 points
Agility . . . . .25 points
Endurance . . . . .20 points

As you can see, this sport is not just about speed. Some of the dogs exhibit tremendous concentration (follow) and are distracted by nothing. Others excel in agility. This is seen when the lure is on a straight path and then abruptly takes a turn. An exceptionally agile dog can take a turn without missing a beat.

The Action

At the start of the course, the hounds that have been selected to run together are each given a blanket of a different color. Their collars are removed and a quick-release collar (known as a sliplead) is substituted. The trio is lined up at the starting line and the owner or handler straddles the dog's back. The Huntmaster confirms that the dogs and the Lure Operator are ready. When the Huntmaster says the "T" sound of "Tally Ho!" the dogs are released (slipped).

Getting ready to slip the hounds.

121

The Lure Operator has an important job because it is up to him to make sure that the lure is just far enough ahead of the dogs so that they don't actually catch it, yet not so far that they lose interest. The Lure Operator must also be ready at a moment's notice to stop the lure should a dog accidentally get caught in the cord.

Most lure courses are between 500 and 1400 yards long. The cord is set out on an irregular course and is run through pulley stakes that are driven into the ground. There are several ways in which a dog can get injured during coursing, although all are relatively rare.

It is possible for a dog to get his foot caught in the cord. That could result in anything from a rope burn to a pulled tendon to a broken bone. Another hazard is that it is possible for dogs to collide. An extreme outcome of that could be a

The chase. (Photo: A. Bruce Lazaravich)

Catching up with the "lure," three white plastic bags.

serious injury, but most likely a bumped dog will simply be thrown off course and lose time (and points).

Check the Dog's Fitness First

Many mishaps can be prevented by ascertaining in advance that your dog is fit to participate. Just as people are advised to check with their physician before starting an exercise program, so, too, should a dog be taken to a veterinarian before you start him coursing. Remember, a dog who is lying

The reward. (Photo: A. Bruce Lazaravich)

on a sofa all week can get just as flabby as a person who does the same. Also, it is essential that you find out why your dog was retired from racing. If it was because he was injured on the track or has a heart or lung problem, then coursing is out! Remember, some injuries don't show until the dog is really active. By then it may be too late.

Always keep in mind that these dogs are retired, and any kind of sport they participate in should be solely for *their* amusement. Of all the sighthound breeds, Greyhounds are the ones that will always run their hearts out, even if it's to the detriment of their health. If your dog seems somewhat lame, if the course is not in perfect condition (hard ground, rutted surface, slippery, etc.) or if the weather is extreme (too hot or too cold or too humid), do your dog a favor and rest him. He'll always want to run, but it's up to you to exercise judgment and caution on his behalf.

Finally, how long you permit your dog to participate in

coursing trials is up to you, but dogs over the age of six may well be considered over the hill for this physically demanding activity. That doesn't mean they're entirely out of the running, though.

One way to enjoy coursing without competing is by attending practice runs set up by your local club. Even older dogs can have fun because you can tell the Lure Operator to take it nice and slow so that your older (or out of shape) dog can still stretch his legs without becoming exhausted. Practice runs are also for dogs that are getting in shape and honing their skills for competitions. At practice runs, a dog can run alone or with a partner of your choice, even with a dog of a different breed.

It is a wonderful sight indeed, at either a practice run or a field trial, to see so many different types of sighthounds gathered in one place with one common purpose. At least half the fun of coursing comes from talking to the other owners and exchanging information about the dogs. The other half of the fun comes from watching the dogs do what they were born to do—run like the wind.

AMATEUR RACING

Another sport limited to sighthounds is oval racing. These events, regulated by the National Oval Track Racing Association (NOTRA), run the dogs on an oval or u-val (U-shaped) track. Greyhounds and Whippets are considered the major breeds, while the other sighthounds are considered minor breeds.

Whippets and the minor breeds use the u-val track while Greyhounds and Whippets use the oval track. The track surfaces are dirt or grass, and great care is taken to make sure they are very level. Continuous loop equipment pulls an artificial lure around the track, and dogs are judged on the order of the finish.

As a dog wins more heats (races) he accumulates more points, which lead to the Oval Racing Championship title (ORC). Points depend not only on where your dog finishes for a day's standing but also on how many other dogs competed that day as well as how many other dogs already have earned an ORC title.

Greyhounds and Whippets must use a starting box for oval racing. They must also be muzzled during the race and know how to use a starting box (no problem for an ex-racer). Because dogs can reach higher speeds on a track than on a lure course, even greater care must be taken to make sure that your dog is fit.

A GREAT JOGGING COMPANION

Another activity that is a natural for Greyhounds is jogging—not alone, of course, but with you. While Greyhounds basically are sprinters, as opposed to long-distance runners, they can build up the necessary endurance if it is done gradually. In fact, the one thing you'll have to watch is that the dog does not try to run too fast and burn himself out. It's a whole different thing for them to learn to lope along. Also, the pads on the dog's feet may be tender, so start out on soft surfaces such as grass.

Whole books have been written on the subject of running with your dog, and you would do well to read at least one of them before you get started. Important health tips are included, as well as information on how to build up your dog's stamina.

Purina has, in recent years, sponsored the Purina Hi Pro

K-9 Fun Run. The specifics of the runs vary from city to city, but they generally feature a one-mile walk/run and, for the more physically fit, a two-mile run. If you and your Greyhound jog together regularly, you both would probably enjoy running with other people and dogs. And imagine your dog's surprise when he realizes that other dogs run, too!

Run for Charity or Fun

Many Greyhound adoption groups hold an annual run for adopters and their dogs. Some do it for the fun of it, while others do it to raise money for the rescue program. If the group you adopted your dog from doesn't have one, why don't you suggest it (and be the one to organize it)?

SHOWING YOUR GREYHOUND

Showing your Greyhound in American Kennel Club-sponsored shows is not an option for two reasons.

First, spayed or neutered dogs do not qualify and your dog almost certainly has been altered. Remember, the purpose of showing is to breed the "best" dogs afterward, and breeding is not the idea behind adopting an ex-racing Greyhound.

Second, it is difficult, and in most cases, impossible, to get the registration papers for your dog. A dog without papers is also ineligible for showing.

There is an alternative, however. My group, Make Peace With Animals, has an annual event called the Greyhound Homecoming, a picnic attended by all of the Greyhounds, accompanied by their new families, that were adopted through us. One popular event during the day is the Dogs of

Distinction ceremony. "Judges" award certificates for such categories as Longest Tail, Biggest Ears, Whitest Teeth, Oldest, etc. The idea, of course, is that all the dogs have something unique to offer and that each one is a winner. And that, too, is the idea behind adopting. Other adoption groups hold similar gatherings and yours can too.

OBEDIENCE TRIALS

Don't be upset about your dog's truncated show career— cheer up! He can still compete in obedience classes. For that you must get an AKC Indefinite Listing Privilege number and proof that the dog has been spayed or neutered.

If you decide to pursue obedience, get a good trainer

The Greyhound Hall of Fame in Abilene, Kansas. (Photo: Greyhound Hall of Fame)

who is both kind *and* who understands retired racers. Greyhounds are a quick study and generally do quite well in obedience.

VISIT THE ELDERLY OR INFIRM

You can have fun with your ex-racer and do a good deed at the same time by taking him to visit hospitals and nursing homes. Many institutions recognize the therapeutic value of such visits. My own adoption group, Make Peace With Animals, has a program called AmbassaDogs®, and we have discovered that, because of their docile nature, Greyhounds are ideal visitors. Two requirements, of course, are that the dogs be housebroken and obedience trained. It is a very moving experience to sit quietly with an older person or someone who is ill, watch them pet a Greyhound and see the joy on their face. Again, if your adoption group doesn't have such a program, why not initiate one?

THE GREYHOUND HALL OF FAME

In Abilene, Kansas (also the home of the National Greyhound Association), there is a museum dedicated to the Greyhound. Any dyed-in-the-wool Greyhound enthusiast must consider this the equivalent of Mecca. While the emphasis is on racing, there are interesting educational exhibits about the history of the breed, as well as examples of art depicting the Greyhound. A side treat is meeting Dutchess, a retired racer who has found a second career as the mascot of the museum.

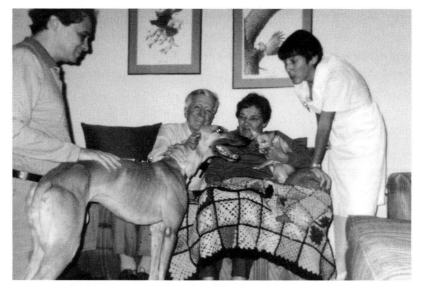

Elderly shut-ins enjoy a visit from Alexandra, a Greyhound, and Paco, a Chihuahua.

SPREAD THE WORD ABOUT ADOPTION

Finally, here is another way to have fun *and* get more people interested in adopting Greyhounds. You will discover very soon after adopting that people will constantly stop you and your dog on the street and say one of two things: "What kind of dog is that? He's so beautiful!" or "Is that one of those racing Greyhounds I've heard about?"

What you can do is this: always be prepared with either a descriptive brochure about adopting or with cards giving the name and number of someone who can be contacted for adoption information. You'll be amazed at the number of people who have always wanted an ex-racing Greyhound but didn't know where to get one. Although it is a lot of fun to sing your dog's praises, Greyhounds, being

130

the wonderful dogs that they are, make even better spokesmen than you could ever be. And remember, for every card or brochure you hand out, there is the possibility that you will have helped a dog in dire need find the loving home he deserves.

APPENDIX
1
OTHER SIGHTHOUNDS

Afghan Hound

Basenji

Borzoi

Ibizan Hound

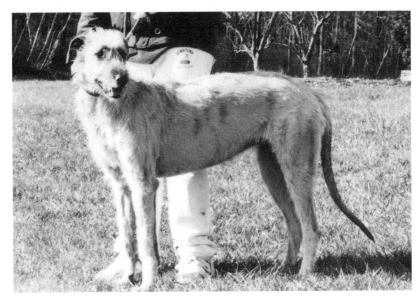

Irish Wolfhound

135

Italian Greyhound

Pharaoh Hound

Rhodesian Ridgeback

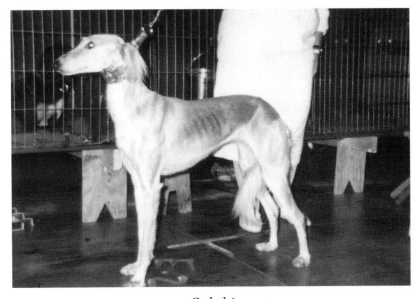

Saluki

Scottish Deerhound

Whippet

APPENDIX

2

THE GREYHOUND'S ANATOMY

////////////

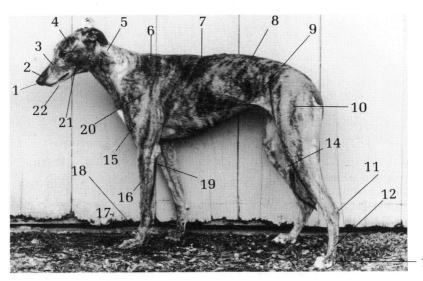

1 Nose.   2 Muzzle.   3 Stop.   4 Apex of skull.
5 Neck.   6 Withers.   7 Back.   8 Hip.   9 Loin.
10 Rump.   11 Hock.   12 Pastern.   13 Toes.   14 Stifle
or knee.   15 Chest.   16 Forearm.   17 Pastern or metacarpus.   18 Wrist or carpus.   19 Elbow.   20 Shoulder.
21 Cheek.   22 Flew.

APPENDIX

3

ADOPTION GROUPS, ORGANIZATIONS AND RESOURCE DIRECTORY

//////////

The following is a list of all known Greyhound adoption groups in the United States and Canada. Inclusion does not signify endorsement.

Fort Myers Greyhound Adoption Center
Donna Forster
11511 Deal Road N.
Fort Myers, FL 33905
813-731-3187

Friends for Life
(an affiliate of California Greyhound Rescue and Northern California Sighthound Rescue)
Susan Netboy
5 Ranch Road
Woodside, CA 94062
415-851-7812

Greyhound Club of America
Cheryl Reynolds, Rescue
  Chairman
4280 Carpenteria Avenue
Carpenteria, CA 93013
805-684-4914

Greyhound Friends, Inc.
Louise Coleman, Director
167 Saddle Hill Road
Hopkinton, MA 01748
508-435-5969

Greyhound Life Line
Irene Milbury
228 E. Foxboro Street
Sharon, MA 02067
617-784-2157

Greyhound Rescue, Inc.
Susan Greenwald
118-B Jordan Court, N.E.
Palm Bay, FL 32905
407-951-2452

Greyhound Rescue, Inc.
John and Denise Davis
6397 Woodburn Road
Elk Ridge, MD 21227
410-796-2803

Greyhounds As Pets
Bill Fullerton
P.O. Box 6999
Colorado Springs, CO 80934
719-633-0171

Greyhound Pets of America
(31 chapters)
Gloria Sanders, President
800-FON 1 GPA
(Your call will be forwarded
to the nearest chapter.)

Greyhound Racers Recycled, Inc.
Jan Huey
Box 270107
Houston, TX 77277-0107
713-665-3366

Greyhound Rescue and Adoption
LaDonna Rea
P.O. Box 461
Plainfield, IN 46168-461
317-745-7772

Greyhound Rescue and Adoption
Linn Murphy
P.O. Box 218205
Columbus, OH 43221-8205
614-777-4160

Greyhound Rescue and Adoption
Beverly Thompson
116 Mary Street
Washington, IL 61571
309-745-5377

Greyhound Rescue League
Paula Johnson
106 Cayman Lane
Summerland Keys, FL 33042
305-872-2749

Greyhound Rescue League of Tallahassee Inc.
Cinda Crawford, Director
P.O. Box 13314
Tallahassee, FL 32317
904-878-1204

Make Peace With Animals, Inc.
Cynthia Branigan, President
P.O. Box 488
New Hope, PA 18938
215-862-0605

Michigan Greyhound Connection
Susan Riegel
797 River Bend Drive
Rochester Hills, MI 48307
313-652-6270

141

National Greyhound Adoption Program
David Wolfe
8301 Torresdale Avenue
Philadelphia, PA 19136
800-348-2517

National Greyhound Network
415-851-7812
(Represents independent groups. You will be referred to the adoption group nearest to you.)

Northern California Sighthound Rescue
Sandra Wornum
570 Riviera Circle
Larkspur, CA 94939
415-924-7020

Operation Greyhound
Bruna Palmatier
8876 Shaula Way
San Diego, CA 92126
619-695-9488

Oregon Greyhound Rescue
Elizabeth Bordeaux
2207 N.E. 79th Avenue
Portland, OR 97213
503-257-7220

Retired Greyhounds As Pets (REGAP)
Ron Walsek
P.O. Box 41307
St. Petersburg, FL 33743
813-347-2206

REGAP of Connecticut, Inc.
Eileen McCaughern
P.O. Box 76
Bethany, CT 06525
203-467-7407

REGAP of Indiana
Sally Allen
1306 Bunker Hill Road
Mooresville, IN 46158
317-996-2154

REGAP of Seabrook, Inc.
Christine Makepeace, Director
P.O. Box 1861
Seabrook, NH 03874
603-474-8340

REGAP of Waterloo
Dale and Jacquie Schnepf
All Pets Animal Clinic
3257 W. 4th Street
Waterloo, Iowa 50701
319-235-0842

Second Chance for Greyhounds
Helen Banks
10826 Dean Street
Bonita Springs, FL 33923
813-947-2365

Tampa Greyhound Adoption Center
Kimberly and Adam Wyler
5629 E. Chelsea Street
Tampa, FL 33610
813-626-1116

Claire Bertine
1000 Reo St. John Drive
Jacksonville, FL 32211
904-743-6627

Richard Benjamin
P.O. Box 397
Beach Island, SC 29842-0397
803-827-0918

Nina Bloom-Selling
4335 E. Carol Ann Lane
Phoenix, AZ 85032
602-493-9144

Pat Lewallen
R.R. 4, Box 232W
Paola, KS 66071
913-294-3023

Diane Lunthacum
Rt. 2, Box 185-C
Thomasville, GA 31742
412-226-7632

Cathy McIntyre
15 Pickering Court #01
Germantown, MD 20874
301-540-4980

Vickey Price
Columbia, SC
803-256-6939 (work)
803-782-0863 (home)

Frank Sawada
6441 Taylor Street
Niagara Falls, Ontario
Canada L2G2E9
416-357-6550

Candy Schultz
Greyhound Pet Connection
Woodstock, IL 60098
815-477-4900 (work)
815-568-8403 (home)

Catherine Settle
P.O. Box 2157
Sanford, NC 27330
919-775-7945

Ellen Stokal
P.O. Box 7044
Villa Park, IL 60181
708-495-0074

Cheryl Vincent
3671 Woodhaven Circle
Hamburg, NY 14075
716-648-8106

Linda Zent
5779 Boxwood Drive
Boseman, MT 59715
406-586-8705

GREYHOUND ORGANIZATIONS

**National Greyhound
Association** (racing
organization and registry)
R.R. 3, Box 111B
Abilene, KS 67410

American Kennel Club (for
registration only)
5580 Centerview Drive
Raleigh, NC 27606

American Kennel Club (main
headquarters)
51 Madison Avenue
New York, NY 10010

Greyhound Club of America
(for AKC-registered
Greyhounds)
4280 Carpenteria Avenue
Carpenteria, CA 93013

GREYHOUND ADVOCACY GROUPS

The Fund for Animals
200 W. 57th Street
NYC, NY 10019

Humane Society of the United States
2100 L Street
Washington, D.C. 20037

In Defense of Animals
816 West Francisco Blvd.
San Rafael, CA 94901

Greyhound Protection League
c/o Palo Alto Humane Society
P.O. Box 60717
Palo Alto, CA 94306

NEAVS (New England Anti-Vivisection Society)
333 Washington Street
Boston, MA 02135

PETA (People for the Ethical Treatment of Animals)
P.O. Box 42516
Washington, D.C. 20015

COURSING/U-VAL RACING

American Sighthound Field Association (artificial lure coursing)
3403 Spinnaker Way
Acworth, GA 30101

National Oval Track Racing Association
540 Glenwood Highway
Goldendale, WA 98620

PUBLICATIONS

The Greyhound Review
(monthly magazine of the
National Greyhound
Association)
R.R. 3, Box 111B
Abilene, KS 67410

National Greyhound Update
(monthly racing magazine)
21684 Granada Avenue
Cupertino, CA 95014

The Sighthound Review (bi-monthly magazine about show
Greyhounds and other
sighthound breeds)
P.O. Box 30430
Santa Barbara, CA 93130

The Windhound (bi-monthly
about all sighthounds, show
and sporting)
Hoflin Publishing, Ltd.
4401 Zephyr Street
Wheat Ridge, CO 80033-3299

ACCESSORIES

Animal Magnetism (mail order, all supplies including specially made coats for Greyhounds, humane choker collars, slip leads for coursing, etc., as well as books and gifts)
P.O. Box 101
Lambertville, NJ 08530

R. C. Steele (mail order, discounted prices on dog crates)
1989 Transit Way, Box 910
Brockport, NY 14420

INDEX

Page numbers in *italics* indicate illustrations.

INDEX